BUNY

BUNYAN OF ELSTOW

Judith Gunn

HODDER AND STOUGHTON
LONDON SYDNEY AUCKLAND TORONTO

British Library Cataloguing in Publication Data

Gunn, Judith
  Bunyan of Elstow.
  1. Bunyan, John—Biography 2. Authors, English—
  Early modern, 1500–1700—Biography
  I. Title
823'.4   PR3331

ISBN 0 340 34823 2

In memory of my Uncle

The Reverend Raymond Price

a fellow Baptist writer

Contents

Preface

John Bunyan was born over three hundred years ago but his name lives on today. Those intervening years have allowed people time to form their own opinions about the man and his actions; numerous academicians have dissected the source material and discussed the what and who and where in detail. From this material and discussion I have written what I imagine to be the life of John Bunyan. I say 'imagine' because, with the passing of time, some of the peripheral details of his life have been lost, or were never documented and imagination must be employed in describing the incidents and individuals of his life, some of whom fade out of his known story, despite their importance, for instance his second wife Elizabeth.

John's life is, to an extent, the story of inner struggle: his conflict of theology as he strives to understand Christianity; and his fight to overcome the depression and terror in the years he spent in gaol.

The Pilgrim's Progress, the book for which he is famous, was his most spectacular success. It is for this that we know him now, but it should not be forgotten that he suffered a great deal in order to establish the principle in this country that a man has a right to speak and believe freely. Without his stand and the years he spent in gaol for that cause, there would have been no *Pilgrim's Progress* and the principle of tolerance that we have today might not have been so easily taken for granted. This biography is not the story of *Pilgrim* but of the man whose life, mind and culture created him.

1

THE BEGINNING OF REVOLUTION

Outside the prison people walked, laughed and worked freely. They drove their horses and carts laden with food, hay and wares to the main market not far away. They stopped beneath the prison windows and shared the news of the day – news from London perhaps, or of the march of the Plague. The people who remained in the cells above often heard snatches of conversation, of laughter, the talk of home, of wives and families and of evening entertainment.

On fine days, the sunlight and warmth would stream through the barred windows of Bedford County Gaol and cheer the prisoners, but on wet and cold days the rain splashed on to the straw bedding and the inmates were miserable and desperate.

Among those who sat or walked restlessly in the confines of the prison was a man in his mid-thirties. He would sit against the wall, sometimes reading, sometimes dreaming. His skin was dull and grey from six years of prison life and he had grown used to the routine. He had disciplined himself to pass the days by making leather Tagg laces to earn some money to help his family. He worked until his fingers ached and trembled, attaching the small metal points to the leather strings, so that they could be stitched into shoes, garments or other articles. It was unfulfilling work, for he could never see the articles that the laces held together. He could only watch as the piles of leather threads were taken away and pray that the money would be enough until he could make some more.

When at last he could rest from the day's tedious work, he would read one of his two books: the Bible, or *Foxe's*

Book of Martyrs. In the latter he found the life stories of
saints who had suffered greatly in the service of their God
and Christianity. Persecuted for their beliefs like him, their
gruesome deaths and suffering had a double effect on him:
sometimes he was strengthened by the evidence of their
fortitude, for compared to theirs his own sufferings seemed
very minor; but at other times he dreaded that perhaps (like
them) the gallows, or worse, was in store for him. He faced
an uncertain future and he often wondered whether he
actually possessed the courage demanded of all martyrs.
Occasionally he was so disturbed and frustrated by his
circumstances, that he could not concentrate on his routine.
His mind kept wandering back to his earliest days, to the
reasons and events that had put him in gaol, into this endless
round of eating, sleeping and waiting. The walls of the prison
were a cage and he paced his cell like an animal.

Now, he could not help but reflect on the freedom he had
lost and he wanted, at last, to record what had brought him
to gaol. He was, after all, an author. He had a readership, a
faithful following and he would tell his story to them. At
least then it would all be explained. Thus, should the worst
happen, should he die a martyr, he would feel purged before
God and the world he knew.

He took up the quill pen and the meagre ink and paper he
had managed to buy with his earnings and donations from
the Church, sat down at the roughly-made table and began
to write.

His mind went first to his trade, to the work that had made
him so strong, healthy, and well able to bear the rigours of
deprivation in prison. Yet he despised being a 'tinker';
despite the poverty of his parents he had been educated and
was self-conscious about his humble beginnings. He looked
at the rough paper on the equally makeshift table and
thought of his childhood and parents, his mother and the
sacrifices that had been made to educate him. It was hard to
know where to begin. It seemed best to get his early life
disposed of quickly for his main interest was his spiritual
development and he saw little connection between that and

his physical development and circumstances. 'For my descent then', he wrote, 'it was as is well known by many, of a low and inconsiderable generation; my father's house being of that rank that is meanest and most despised of all the families of the land'.

John Bunyan's father had also been a tinker. The reputation of tinkers, or braziers, was a bad one, mainly because it was a job usually associated with gypsies, who were social outcasts. It suited a traveller's life (in the course of their wanderings) to mend kettles and do iron-work because it was the kind of work that was always available and easily done in the villages and towns they came to. However, John's family were never gypsies, and the Bunyans were, on the whole, a respectable family. A few centuries before they had been yeomen farmers, but as time went on they suffered losses and turned to tinkering in order to hold on to their home and their last small field. Admittedly one ancestor had been hanged in 1219, but there was no real blot upon the family name.

Thomas Bunyan was twenty-six when his first child, John, was born. He had been married once before and widowed, so the sight of his second wife, Margaret, in labour was frightening to this young but hopeful man. The labour, however, was without complications and to their relief no 'Childbed Fever' (a common infection which was the cause of death of many a new mother until the late nineteenth century) or haemorrhage followed. Thomas was overjoyed as his indignant son roared his first comment to the world. It was the autumn of 1628.

Few parents (whatever they may hope) as they observe their screaming infants or muddied toddlers expect their children to make a mark upon history that will not fade, but John Bunyan, now showing little potential in his mother's arms, was not only to live a life that would span one of the most important and exciting times in English history, but he was to play an influential part in that era, and beyond.

Three years before John's birth, Charles I had come to the throne. He began his reign convinced, like many before him,

that God had given him the Divine Right to reign. This
'right' meant to the King that he was God's representative on
earth. Just as God had chosen King David to rule over the
Israelites, he, Charles, had been chosen to rule over England
and no one should question this, nor even his methods. To
do so would be to defy God and risk death in the Tower and
eternal damnation. Charles, as the King, was answerable to
no one but God and therefore, if he so wished, he could rule
without consulting Parliament and from 1629 (just a few
months before John's birth) that is just what he did, for
eleven fatal years.

John's christening was registered simply enough in the
parish records: 'John the sonne of Thomas Bonnion Jun; 20
November'. His home was a small two-roomed cottage that
had once seen better days. Thomas and his wife worked hard
to keep the cottage and their smallholding, but their efforts
were not always appreciated by their son. John's self-
consciousness about his family's profession was probably
born in his early school days. To have a father who was a
tinker was a subject for ridicule amongst the better-off
children who more commonly attended school. John
absorbed their attitudes: his education took him beyond the
class of his parents, but it did not give him the wisdom to
honour them and their work. While they worked, John
studied. He did not, however, learn Latin and could not
therefore be considered, by contemporary standards, to be
truly educated. Nevertheless, to be able to read and write was
quite an achievement for the son of such a poor family. It can
have been no small sacrifice on the part of his parents to
provide for his education, for they would have had to go
without the money that the young John might well have
earned helping his father.

All through his childhood the political situation grew
worse. The years of tyranny and muted rebellion brought
about much radical thought that was soon to be voiced in a
recalled Parliament. The King had an ally in the form of his
appointee, the Archbishop of Canterbury, William Laud;
even post-Reformation, the Archbishop was still second

only to the King in status. Laud tried to prevent dissent in the Church (which might have been dangerous to the King as well as to himself) by insisting that the Common Prayer Book be the only form of worship used in church services. The clergy could no longer arrange their own forms of worship, but had to adhere to a strict form of ritual that would make uniform every church service in the land, thereby allowing no possible heresy or political comment. This action provoked, rather than prevented, further dissent and at last Charles decided to recall Parliament, where an angry clergy took its opportunity to introduce an Act that would abolish the Church hierarchy. Ministers, deans, bishops and, of course, the Archbishop himself, would all be removed if the dissenting clergy were to have their way. This Parliament, however, came to an ignominious end and was dissolved before it could get much further. Again the country heaved with resentment at the King's pre-emptive and tyrannical behaviour. Despite the worsening situation most people, including the schoolboy John, were unaware that Charles was hurtling his country towards revolution and the most daring judicial murder in history.

It was not only in England that political controversy raged; Europe had erupted into the vicious and barbaric Thirty Years War. This conflict was notorious for its atrocities and violence and although communication was limited, rumours of its horrors filtered back (ever exaggerated like Chinese Whispers) to England. In Elstow, while John tried to study, he heard the stories of torture and terror, of massacre and religious persecution. Although Elstow itself was peaceful enough, it was separated from this violence only by a thin stretch of water and the possibility of a similar ugly war occurring in England must have seemed ominously real.

International and national events were not the only sources of disturbance in young John's mind. In a book written some thirty years later, he tells a story through one of his characters which has the authenticity of an eye-witness account. It happened when he was about ten years old and clearly had a profound effect on him.

There was an old man living in the village who suffered from fits. John himself had seen this man in the throes of a convulsion. The villagers believed (and so did John) that a demon was hiding in a large lump on the old man's neck. No doubt this man suffered a great deal; not just from the physical ailments that afflicted him, but from the suspicion and mistrust of his fellow villagers who believed him to be possessed by the Devil.

Eventually the sight of this man and his fits became too much for his neighbours and they decided to take action. They surrounded him and took him to an inn where John, unseen, witnessed what happened next. From the best of intentions the villagers persuaded a Freeman (a kind of doctor) to help them. Under his direction they forced the man to lie on his stomach on a trestle table, with his head hanging over smoking coals, which they held under his mouth. The idea was to smoke the demon out. The man choked and squirmed on the table struggling for breath; perhaps he too believed in the possibility of such a cure or perhaps he was forced unwilling to suffer as he did. Whatever his choice, he nearly died of the treatment and no devil retreated from him. At last John was spotted by the villagers and sent home. The man himself very soon died.

It is small wonder, then, that in such an atmosphere the little boy was terrified by nightmares and visions of hell. He was surrounded by superstition, by the seventeenth-century attitude of personifying evil and the supernatural. Punishment for crime was harsh, such as flogging or hanging. At the church he saw the stone gargoyles, fearsome in their appearance, glaring outwards to ward off the evil eye. These images haunted him, as did the powerful descriptions of hell and the suffering of the damned in the lake of fire. All this was believed literally by the people who populated John's world and left the small child in a nightmare hell of his own. At night he dreamed that the evil figures attacked him, dragging him down into hell. So convinced was he of the reality of these dreams that even in church he trembled for fear that the gargoyles would swoop upon him and drag him off. Sometimes he thought he saw them move. He visualised the torments of hell so vividly that he could almost smell the sulphur and he was so sure of his damnation that he began to wish he was a demon, for surely those who torment are not themselves tormented?

Despite the penalty for not attending church – a fine of one shilling for every service not attended unless genuine sickness could be proved, a fine worth, in present terms, perhaps forty pounds – John was not a religious boy; he romped and played with the local boys and inevitably got into scrapes. He feared hell, but had no wish to become a monk or a pious soul in order to avoid it. He had little thought of heaven or of gaining access to it. He was a growing boy, lively and mischievous; life was too much fun to spoil with what he saw as religious austerity and self-sacrifice.

He and his friends played hard when the opportunity arose. At the back of Elstow, not a few hundred yards from John's house, there was a small stream: a source of water for the village and a source of entertainment for the children. Fishing was a favourite sport, but as John grew older the small fry to be caught in the relatively harmless stream lost their interest for him. The fishing to be had in the River Ouse was much more exciting. This river, running through Bedford, certainly had larger fish and more attractions for a group of boys than the stream, but it also held more dangers. It is not in the nature of little boys to temper their enthusiasm with caution and John was to learn the lesson of the dangerous water the hard way.

He and his friends had been given permission to take a boat out on the Ouse and like most of their contemporaries not one of them could swim. Nevertheless, undaunted, they pushed the boat from the bank, fishing sticks and twine at the ready. They rowed out until they were as far from either bank as they could be and, satisfied that they were now beyond adult intervention, they began fishing. How it actually happened John does not explain, but in the scramble for lines and sticks, perhaps as a result of the twitch of a fish on one of the lines, John fell in. He sank quickly into the depths of the black water, the weight of his clothes pulling him down. He struggled to the surface, splashing and pushing against the water, reacting more from instinct than skill. He choked and retched as the water filled his mouth, he felt dizzy and stunned. He could feel the demons he had dreamt of tugging at his feet and dragging him into hell. He scraped his hands against the rough side of the boat, other hands were reaching out to him. He grasped one and felt the demons at his feet begin to give way. Choking and vomiting he was dragged into the boat, where he lay on the bottom, bruised and exhausted. The boys rowed to the bank, subdued at least for the rest of that day.

This early brush with death did not sober John for long. But his fear of hell began to fade as he approached his adolescence, and the earthly cares of living in seventeenth-century England dominated his life and thoughts. The future looked uncertain, for what would the world want with an educated tinker? John sought the esteem of his colleagues at school. He could not conceal the self-consciousness he had about his background and he worked hard to be popular with his contemporaries. Occasionally he was a little foolhardy in his attempts to impress his friends. One day he risked his life.

He and a friend were walking one afternoon through a field; it was a hot summer's day. There, on the path before them, lay an unsuspecting adder basking in the sun. The snake was quite oblivious to the two youths until John leant down and caught it behind the head, grinning at his friend for approval. Carefully, but still at great risk to himself, he set about removing the adder's sting, its poison sac. 'I might by my own foolishness have put an end to myself there and then,' said John ruefully, when he recalled the event twenty years later. He felt that these incidents were sent by God to remind him of his own mortality and ultimate fate, but he was never daunted for long. For a young man, then very afraid of hell, he certainly seemed to want to hurry his way into it.

In 1643 however, John's carefree childhood was to end abruptly. Already, for a year, the country had been torn apart by Civil War. The King had levied an illegal tax, Ship Money, the assessments for which were so heavy that some counties refused to pay it. Bedford, John's own county, was among the leading five counties that defaulted on the tax and when Parliament was re-elected, Bedford returned four MPs loyal to the cause of Parliament rather than to the King. In 1642 the King had been forced to retreat to Nottingham and raise his standard there, thus declaring war on his own people. From Nottingham he tried to rule over his divided country, but a new Parliamentary army arose, and a new leader, Oliver Cromwell, began to make his mark.

While the country battled against itself, the turmoil of England was reduced to small proportions compared to the tragedy that took place in John's life. In June, when he was fifteen, a strange illness swept the village taking his young sister and his mother with it. They died within a month of each other and John's heartbreak at this loss could not have been eased by the sight of his father bringing home a new wife in August of that year, just three months after the death of his mother. Perhaps with a number of small children to look after and feed, Thomas had married to provide a nursemaid as well as a wife, but in the eyes of his son he was a lecherous old fool. So, early in 1644, John left his childhood behind him and went to serve with Parliament's forces in the New Model Army that now fought the King.

2

ACTIVE SERVICE

No one would have thought, just a few years before, that the English people would defy the authority of the King to the point of war. England, where the monarchy had always seemed so secure, was battling to topple an institution as well as a man. The two sides that now lined up against each another found themselves surprised by war. They had entered into battle more by coincidence than intention and so were unprepared.

When a country raises an army to fight against another country such as Spain or France, the armies raised are in some ways trained for war. In the case of Civil War it was different. The people had a choice as to which side they should join, and because they volunteered, they approached the war with enthusiasm but not discipline, skirmishing and withdrawing, rather than attacking with the confidence of true men of war.

Each side, however amateur, fundamentally believed in the rightness of its cause. The Royalists believed that the King had absolute power vested in him by God. The Parliamentarians believed that the King so badly abused this power that he blasphemed with it and had to be stopped. Every man who fought, on whatever side, believed he was fighting a Holy War.

So it was a largely makeshift army that John joined. There were a very few professional soldiers; for the rest there were squires, lawyers and a few tinkers like himself. It was a dedicated army but it lacked skill and it was this shortcoming that Oliver Cromwell saw and dealt with, quickly and efficiently. The methods he used no doubt influenced the young John and grounded him in the developing tradition of Puritanism.

'No man swears but he pays 12 pence; if he be drunk he is set in the stocks or worse!', stated a report in a 1643 local newspaper. Cromwell's efforts to train his ragbag of men had attracted attention. However dedicated the men were, obedience and discipline were sometimes overwhelmed by the temptations of drink and other vices. The Puritans were setting the ground rules for a new way of life and such vices were not tolerated in their army. Cromwell not only punished his men for the more common misdemeanours but also for the more unusual. A man was instantly cashiered if he referred to his own side as the 'Roundheads', the name by which they had become known in the country because of their round helmets, and the name by which history remembers them. Cromwell was concerned not only for discipline but for morale and mutual respect. He felt his army had a sacred duty to perform and they had to be worthy of it. The New Model Army, as it became known, was in training not only for physical warfare but for spiritual warfare. Each man carried a Bible, and they studied the word of God around the fire at night. They were encouraged to discuss and interpret what they read, and in particular they tried to relate it to their own situation. In this atmosphere new ideas and theologies flourished. Itinerant preachers travelled round the various camps, preaching from the scriptures. The New Model Army soon became famous for its preachers and its Bible studies around the fire. In fact it was the hope of their enemy that the various ideas preached would divide the Puritans against each other and cause their defeat.

Suddenly flung into a world of adults and war, the adolescent John heard and saw this revival of thought and faith. During those war years, people talked of equality, of levelling all property and holding it in common, of the redistribution of wealth, of people's committees and of justice in the land. The preachers abhorred Papism. They condemned the rituals of the Anglican Church. There would be no more Common Prayer Book, no more sheep-like chanting. Ideas and thoughts were planted like seeds in the minds of the listeners round the fires, who pored over their Bibles before the battles of the day. John was one of these and although he was involved fully in army life, like most of his contemporaries his acceptance of the faith was superficial. He co-operated both because it was a socially acceptable thing to do and because the threat of punishment if he failed was a reasonable incentive.

It was during this time that John first came across William Dell. Dell was Cromwell's favoured preacher and he travelled the country encouraging the troops in the faith. He possessed a great gift of preaching that rarely failed to touch his listeners. John, however, remained unmoved, unaware of how important a friend William Dell would later become.

So despite the heavy indoctrination of the New Model Army, John was not convinced and did not consider himself in need of the love of God. He still grieved for his mother and sister and his father's apparent betrayal of them all. He held God responsible for this and could not bring himself near to someone who seemed so unmerciful.

Instead John set himself to the task of training for action. He would forget his childhood and live the independent life of the man he aspired to be. He spent two years in the army but in that time saw very little action and some of that was of his own making. Still fascinated by water and the sport of fishing, John came to grief again following this pastime. This time he fell into an estuary on the coast. Luckily, he was not alone and was hauled out by his companions. Once again John had been warned by providence of the mortality of his body, but once again he was not seriously concerned by the incident.

At last his platoon was called to action. It was a blessing for John for, preoccupied with activity, he could forget the grief and anger that haunted him. As they approached Leicester to join the siege of the city, John's excitement and apprehension increased. His imagination was as active as it had been in his childhood. He anticipated the future action with as much fervour and fear as he had once imagined the terrors of hell. He had a greatly accentuated sense of the correct way to behave (something which he felt his father failed to do) and despite his fears he would stand firm. Not only that, in his better moments, he realised that here was an opportunity for advancement. It was a chance for him and his colleagues to distinguish themselves from the crowd and the humdrum poor existence they had lived until that moment.

He had been detailed to go out with a group to the front line on some kind of sortie. He was not told the objective, nor what he would be doing, and was almost ready to go when a friend came to him and asked if he would swap duties with him. John was too relieved to ask why, and made no objection. He wished the man luck and watched him go, only gradually becoming aware of a feeling of anti-climax. He wondered whether he had done the right thing, the honourable thing. He was glad the evil hour had been delayed but restless at the endless inertia. Anything would be better than worrying and waiting.

At last the detail returned and to John's dismay they carried with them one body, the body of the man who had taken his duty. When he had arrived at the front line he had been ordered to stand guard. Exposed, perhaps inattentive, he was shot by a single musket bullet that drilled through his helmet and penetrated his skull. He died instantly.

John often spoke of this event later, to illustrate how near to death every man is. At the time, it only served to expose warfare for what it was, a dangerous tragic affair. The war and the army no longer seemed the safe haven from the loss of his childhood security that he had initially hoped for and found.

The first round of the Civil War was drawing to a close. The King had been forced to negotiate and although he and his army were to make one last bid for the Divine Right to rule (in 1647) John had no interest in staying on and seeing the thing through to its conclusion. He had learned and seen enough of action to record it some thirty years later in his

book *The Holy War*, an allegorical story of the siege of
Mansoul. It was a sufficiently vivid memory for him to
mould one of the characters on an officer he had come
across, but for now enough was enough.

Moreover, John had taken a further step towards
manhood. He had met a young woman, Mary. She came to
him alone, with no parents and little in the way of money or
material goods. The memory of her father (possibly killed in
the war) was still fresh in her mind and she often spoke of
him to John. He had been a good and holy man and she
would have hoped for as much from her husband. Aware of
this, John returned to Elstow to announce to his father his
intention to marry and to try to build up enough business to
make marriage a practical project. John's father had little to
say in the matter and John himself had little respect for his
father's opinion, so Mary came unopposed to Elstow. She
found her new father welcoming but cautious of his son's
brittle temper and moods.

It was the start of a new and uncertain era, both in the life
of the newly-weds and in the times of the country.

3

VISIONS

The couple settled down to a sparse married life and slightly
uncomfortable family relationships. They had not married
in Elstow; John had disappeared one day, announcing his
intention of marrying Mary and bringing her home.

He was hardly ready to keep a wife. He was not even
twenty and he had refused help from his father and his
stepmother for he was determined to establish himself
independently. He had made a few of his own tools including
the iron anvil he carried. This outsized nail was nine or so
inches in diameter at the top and tapered to a point at the
bottom. He scratched the words 'J. Bunyan' up the side so
that there could be no confusion with his father's tools, and
he made a sling to carry it. He carried his tools and the anvil
around the lanes and streets of Elstow and Bedford,
becoming a familiar figure in the area. He was tall and
muscular, even though he still had some growing to do; he
was approaching the full strength of his manhood and his
flash of red hair made him more noticeable. Hard and well
built, his brazier's arms already bulging with strength,
tanned and weatherbeaten, he wandered the area calling out
his trade and seeking work. When he got some he shoved the
point of the anvil into the ground and worked on the top.
What work he could not do *in situ* he brought back to the
forge he had built next to his two-roomed cottage, of which
he was very proud.

He was well aware, however, that the cottage was no
palace. There was a small table and a few pots and pans that
had been discarded by their previous owners and which John

had rescued and mended. In time there would be more furniture and more comfort, but for Mary starting a new life in a strange village there was little to encourage her.

It was not an easy life and after school and active service John felt his future was very bleak. Mary was the only advent in his life that saved his prospects from looking totally desolate. He tried to compensate for his disillusion by flinging himself enthusiastically into the social life of the village.

Like most English villages, Elstow possessed a church with a bell tower. John loved to hear the bells ringing out the changes and he soon learned to ring them himself. He would meet his fellow campanologists in the evenings and they would chat, decide on the evening's ringing and begin. This was at a time when social barriers could drop slightly, friendships could be established and he could forget the stigma he felt he carried in the anvil on his back. He concentrated hard once the ringing began, for the peals satisfied his urge to make something good. Above him he could hear the bells booming one, two, three and down! He pulled on his own rope and despite the deafening resonance of the other bells he could always hear his own singing out its message to the countryside. He often wondered how far the sound could carry and he adored it when sometimes, returning from Bedford, he heard his bells calling to him. Full of energy and strength John out-rang his fellows, and it always seemed too soon when they stopped for the night. His momentary disappointment found compensation in a drink in the inn in the company of his bell-ringing friends. He returned home late at night to find his wife, sometimes in bed, sometimes waiting up for him and his pangs of guilt did not always make him kind to her.

In his second hobby though, Mary could take more part, for dancing was another pastime that John eagerly followed. He and Mary would hurry to the green on summer nights or to a barn in the winter and dance and laugh with the other people in the village. John, always over-enthusiastic, would take every opportunity to wear himself out and Mary with him. He liked it best when he was exhausted, unable to think or speculate about the future. If Mary grew tired then John could laugh and revel with Harry, who became his closest and most indispensable friend – at least for a time.

John had settled into the mould of English country life. The nation itself still heaved and twitched as the monarchy died and King Charles I faced his trial with a stubborn refusal to recognise its authority. His unshakeable belief in the reality of the Divine Right of Kings to rule brought about his own death and a republic in England, a radical step that has never since been repeated.

While life became a feverish round of drinking, dancing and bell-ringing for John, Mary remained at home. She made a few friends in the village, but as with most women of her time it was as much as she could do to hold their small home together and keep up with the pace that John set. He required a great deal of patience, had a volatile temper and a foul mouth. He was eager for laughter and pranks and all sport attracted him. He jumped at any chance to be with his friends and prove himself worthy of them. Occasionally, attracted by Mary's serenity, he would sit with her in the cottage and bathe in her calm self-assured faith. Mary still spoke of her father and of his piety and faith, a faith which she shared. She had inherited from him only two books, best-sellers of their time: *The Practice of Piety* and *The Plain Man's Pathway to Heaven* by Arthur Dent. Sometimes they would read these books together, with John sitting at her feet reading the stories to her. On cold winter's nights they found the story of a hot day in May in *The Plain Man's Pathway* strangely comforting. It told of four men, a divine, a caviller, an honest man and an ignorant man. These four sat beneath a tree and watched the festivities of May Day pass while they talked of heaven and hell and of piety. They discussed the nature of these concepts and thus, through them, their author moralised. The images danced before the couple's eyes and John was pleased by the story. He was always glad when Mary finally did persuade him to slow down and be with her.

Gradually Mary influenced her husband and began to guide him towards the Church. John started to go on a more regular basis, twice a Sunday in fact, rather than the statutory once. He sang and prayed as lustily as his neighbours but he maintained his life of games, swearing and dancing. John was taking out an insurance policy against the possibility of going to hell. Hell, that old spectre of his childhood dreams, still haunted him and it was believed absolutely by most of his friends. Only Harry seemed untouched by his fears and laughed nervously at his friend's new-found piety. But the stories in Mary's books re-awakened his fears and John fought them off by holding the cross before himself against the vampire of his terror.

As with everything, John became over-enthusiastic. He adored not only the Church, but the priests, their clothes, the extras that attended the Anglican Church, still heavily influenced by the traditions of Rome. John's attitude towards the clergy was obsequious. Despite the contradictions of his life he feigned so great a love of the clergy that he convinced himself it was genuine. He was, after all, attentive enough to the sermons and listened with deep concentration to what was said. His attention was caught by references in the Bible to the 'Chosen Race'. Even though he still disliked his father, there were few other people to go to on matters of religion, so reluctantly one day he approached his father on the subject. He assumed that his father by reason of his age would have the answer.

'Have you heard of the Chosen Race?' John asked as he was helping his father with a job that required two pairs of hands. His father paused and reached for a bottle resting on the ground. He drank deeply and looked thoughtful. 'Yes, it's in the Bible,' he said at last.

'Yes, but who are they?' pressed John.

'The Jews, I think.'

'The Jews – not us?' John frowned. He was puzzled by God's apparent favouritism.

'Yes, or the Israelites at least,' his father went on. 'The story goes that God chose them to be His people from the beginning of time.'

'So we are not the Chosen Race, because we're Gentiles.'

'I think not, not in the strictest sense.'

They returned to their work, but John was mystified. If God had already chosen a race to save then why were they all trying so hard to be saved, when God had his eyes elsewhere? John found the rituals fascinating but the restrictions irksome and part of him was looking for a way out, for a chance to say that he could not save his soul, so why should he bother to try? The realisation that he was not of the Chosen Race seemed to be the answer, but for Mary's sake more than anything he continued rather half-heartedly seeking out the truth. Mary's own patient piety steadied him, so that he did not abandon religion altogether.

One Sunday, as was their usual habit, the couple set out to the church. The weather was bright and warm and John did not relish the thought of the church service he was about to attend; it was a day for fishing not for listening. Nevertheless John found himself sitting through a sermon that for the first time really began to prick his conscience. The vicar spoke against frivolous behaviour. He attacked sport, drinking and the pleasures of the flesh. John began to think the vicar was preaching specifically at him and he started to feel uncomfortable. He was struck again with the fear of hell and for the first time he felt an inkling that his own life was not lived in the way that God would demand of those who wished for salvation. Perhaps there was, after all, a way to God without being a member of the Chosen Race; why else would the vicar preach so hard? Worried by the sermon, John went home to consider what had been said.

Mary soon raised her husband's spirits with her own good cooking. She reassured her husband, hesitantly, that the vicar was not actually getting at him personally. Elated that he no longer felt guilty, John put the sermon out of his mind, kissed Mary quickly to say thank you for the lunch and then, leaving her alone, went back to the village green for a game of Cat.

'Hello, John,' called the team that he had seen gathering from his cottage window. He hurried to join them, cutting a boyish figure as he greeted his friends; he seemed hardly old

enough to be a married man. He picked up his bat of wood
with which to belt the Cat (Cat being a game much like
Rounders, but played with sticks instead of balls). They set
up the teams, laughing. The warmth of activity, the strength
of his own body pleased him. 'Hoy, John! Give it a belt ...
that's it.' He walloped the stick towards his friends and
laughed as they scrambled after it. He ran, charging round
the pitch, to wait for another chance.

He had not had more than one go and was about to take a
second swipe at the Cat when he heard his name called.
'John, John!' The voice was audible, a real voice. He looked
round for its source, but no one had spoken. 'John!' It came
from above. He looked up and froze. There to his terror was
a vision of Christ, glaring at him, not pleased. 'John,' He
repeated. 'Will you leave your sins and go to heaven, or have
your sins and go to hell?' John met the eyes of a severe Christ
and felt the premonition of punishment. His heart went cold,
the Cat fell uselessly at his feet, his face was grey and he
trembled as if about to faint. His friends stared at him. Was
he ill?

John was a fast thinker though, and he still clung to his
worldly pleasures. No sooner had he understood the
implications of what he had just seen and heard than he
decided that he was already beyond hope. Jesus was clearly
angry with him. This was not a warning, a chance to repent,
but a statement of excommunication. He was damned for
ever for his frivolous ways. Thus John reasoned, and having
decided that, he continued with the game shaken, but
undeterred. If he was damned already he would play on and
enjoy the life he lived now, for he would certainly pay for it in
hell. Nevertheless the enjoyment of the day was curtailed.

John could not face the thought of hell without bitterness
and a sense of injustice. He felt himself to be an outcast, no
one could offer him comfort and in a kind of hateful spite he
decided to sin to the full and taste the sweetness of it all
before he died.

Elstow was a small village and John an energetic man. He
says little of his wife, but she suffered a good deal at the

hands of his subsequent selfish behaviour. What had seemed
to be progress had now turned to regression and he made life
lonely for her with his nights at the inn and general revelry.
The neighbours watched his activities with disapproval. The
lonely wife was left at home while her husband spent more
and more time in the inn and staggered home late, resenting
the restrictions that his early marriage had put upon his
enjoyment. His abusiveness grew worse and his neglect of
her hurt deeply, although she was careful to be kind and
unprovocative in her reproaches. She, after all, had nowhere
else to go, no other means of survival.

John would have his readership believe that he was a most
evil character then, but he was never unfaithful to Mary, nor
directly cruel. Nevertheless he carried the guilt of those days
within him for the rest of his life.

This spell of ruthless vice did not last long though.
However reprehensible it seemed to the older John, it did
come to an abrupt and amusing end. He had been behaving
in his usual incorrigible manner outside a friend's shop. He
was looking in at the shop window, swearing at the prices
and the shoddy workmanship of the goods for sale.
Suddenly an old woman flew out of a nearby door at him.
She herself was no paragon of virtue, known in the village as
a woman of ill repute. Her looks had long since been marred
by disease and hard work. She had seen evil, but she was
shocked to hear John swear as he did. 'How dare you?' she
shouted. 'How dare you? Who do you think you are?' her
voice reached a higher level than John had previously
thought possible of the human vocal chords. He was stunned
into silence by the sight of this angry harridan attacking him
with everything but a rolling pin. 'What right have you to
pollute the air with your foul tongue? It makes me tremble to
hear you. You must be possessed by the very Devil himself,
for where else would you learn such filth but in hell? You
could corrupt the whole town with a mouth like that and I
dread to think what you do to the young people in your
earshot. You're the most ungodly wretch I've had the
misfortune to meet, and believe me I've seen a few. You're

old enough to know better and I don't want to hear or see
you ever again. At least I don't want to hear that foul mouth
of yours ever again.'

John became the object of some mockery when the old
woman stamped away. His humiliation had been observed
and it was all he could do to mumble an apology and hurry
away, stung into shame and despair. He was now convinced
of his damnation and very much ashamed of his sin. He said
little to Mary that night. She had heard of the incident but
resisted the temptation to reproach him further or say 'I told
you so'. John had been flung into one of his despairing
moods. He wished that night, more dearly than anything,
that he could be a child again; that he could tread a different
path in growing up and never learn to swear. Suddenly he
seemed to himself to be a most desperate and evil man, but
there was no way of escaping from his weakness and sin. He
was doomed, not worthy of God or heaven.

4

THE BEDFORD CONGREGATION

The change in John, after the incident over his bad language, was immediate. He took the criticism very seriously; although he was reckless with his own soul, he did not want to be reponsible for someone else's downfall. It was a relief to him to discover that the image of the tough, swearing man was not necessarily an impressive one, so he gave up the effort willingly. This change in character did, in fact, have the effect on his fellows that he had sought so hard: they were impressed. His friends and neighbours began to encourage him, ask after his health, say good morning and not scurry by for fear of a sharp word or a crude retort. At last John was gaining the respect of his contemporaries.

But the change was a change of behaviour and not a change of heart. John was still a boisterous and over-energetic man. He continued to bell-ring and dance and visits to the inn were still very much a part of his life. He still admired his friend Harry and he wanted to do nothing that would jeopardise that friendship.

It was growing generally more difficult to be a 'happy-go-lucky Jack the lad' for Puritan England was becoming austere. It was not as easy as it once was to throw caution to the wind and dance the night away. Theatres and inns were closing down, sport was frowned upon and the pleasures of the flesh disdained. People began to wear the sombre greys and blacks favoured by the Puritans; alcohol was the spirit of the Devil; dancing was the sport of the Devil for it could so easily lead to illicit sex, the ultimate crime! John's pastimes were becoming unpopular, they did not fit in with the new

conformity. Even the Church did not escape. The rituals of
the services and the colours of the costumes of the priests
(which John so loved and which made the Church bearable
for him) were denounced by the Puritans as little less than
Papist. John was in the minority.

With the demise of pleasure and Anglican conformity
new ideas found voice. Each man had the right to direct
communication with God. There was no need for the
Common Prayer Book, whose words were merely an empty
chant and nothing compared to the thoughts and feelings of
the individual finding his own voice in prayer. It was now
much easier for people to discuss their doubts and concerns
about the things of God openly and not be accused of heresy.
The whole country became a kind of New Model Army
gathered round the fire at night, discussing God and religion.

It was in this atmosphere that John met an elderly man
who had found a new interest in life since the new regime had
allowed him to approach the Bible with a greater freedom.
He could view it with new eyes, voice thoughts that he had
once smothered, make interpretations that were once
considered heresy. It was an exciting age and the old man
grabbed its opportunities with enthusiasm and began to
share his new-found freedom with John.

The old man lived alone and John and Mary often asked
him round to lunch after church on a Sunday and it was then
that they talked. During these sessions, after a good meal,
the old man became animated. He would take his well-
thumbed Bible and read from St Paul. He seemed to live
through the apostle's experience and understood Paul's
mind as if he had known the man himself. His perceptions
began to interest John and for the first time he saw the Bible,
not as a book full of disapproving notions, but as a record of
adventure, spiritual courage and wisdom. The old man's
excitement was catching and he began to communicate to
John a genuine interest in the Christian religion.

The readings had some effect and John began to curb his
rather more extreme behaviour. He read of how Paul had led
a life full of bitterness and sin, of how he had persecuted the

people of God and yet God had not only saved him, but sought him out to do so! Perhaps, then, there was hope for John who had thought himself beyond salvation. He started trying to keep the commandments and claimed some success, although his relationship with his father still proved a stumbling block sometimes. He fell into the habit of confession and repentance. When he sinned he said 'sorry' and promised to try not to do it again. He was sure now that he was pleasing to God. He was certainly pleasing to his fellow men who now considered him popular and likeable. In fact, they were so amazed by the continued improvement that they remarked that it was as if 'Tom of Bedlam' was changed to a sober man. John had appeared to have gone through a 'Damascus road' experience and seen the light. Nevertheless, impressive though the change was, it remained a partial metamorphosis; he still could not conform to the atmosphere of piety in which he lived. He could stop swearing but not dancing, he would behave politely, but he could not believe in God's grace. He did not understand yet what he finally came to understand, that God's salvation did not depend on his behaviour.

Then came the first indication of the tumultuous doubts and fears that were to attack him in the coming months, and drag him through to a full understanding of the faith he was pursuing. John had rebelled against the atmosphere of the new Puritan Republic and against the austere cultural revolution that was taking hold of the country, but it was beginning to undermine his self-assurance. Bell-ringing suddenly appeared to him to be a pursuit that God would frown upon. It was an activity which, to John, was pure pleasure and somehow he felt that God had not created him to enjoy himself. Week after week since he had returned to Elstow he had joined his fellow villagers in the Bell Tower, ringing out the changes, but the newly pious John now struggled against the feeling that such activities were vain.

He sought advice from the old man who had become his spiritual counsellor but he replied seriously with the then accepted line, that pleasure was evil as it diverted one's

thoughts from God. It took away man's ability to
concentrate on what God willed and the good works He had
set aside for each man. There was too much for each man to
do in the world without wasting time on fripperies. John
could find nothing in the Bible to indicate whether or not he
should continue with bell-ringing. The prevailing attitude,
though, was very much against such activities, for all trivial
enjoyment was reminiscent of the monarchists and Royal-
ism. In addition, because of the bell-ringing John still
suffered some disapproval from his neighbours and,
conscious of his lower social standing, this became more
than he could bear. So, at last, he decided to give up his
favourite pastime – but it was easier decided than done. He
loved it so much that he could not bring himself to stay away
for long. To the surprise of his friends he took to standing in
the Bell Tower to look on while they continued to ring.

Then the old hellish nightmares of his childhood returned.
Just as the gargoyles of the church had haunted the boy and
threatened to drag him into hell, so the adult began to fear
that the bells of the tower would fly off their beams and fall
on to him, providing a fitting punishment for a man who still
looked longingly upon his renounced sin. John took to
standing beneath the main beam to gain some protection
from the flying bell. But then he imagined that should the
murderous bell fly off and hit the wall first, it could re-bound
under the beam and still kill him. So John took to standing
in the doorway of the Bell Tower so he could escape the
falling bell. Then John imagined the whole steeple collapsing
under the power of the possessed bell. Thus tormented by his
irrational fear, John no longer went to hear the bells ring,
but sat and worked at home, listening to the chimes and
fighting his guilt and longing.

The power of this fear in the adult John was an
overwhelmingly neurotic one, like a gnawing pain, and this
was just the beginning of John's almost manic despair and
desperate guilt. He had been captured by the Giant Despair
and suffered the torment of its prison, about which many
years later, he was to write.

He swung between feelings of pious pride, when he had achieved something that he thought would please God, and despair and guilt when he remembered his failings. It took him another year to give up dancing and that was, no doubt, accompanied by the same internal wrangling, but at last he did it, perhaps encouraged by the growing austerity around him.

John assessed his progress as a Christian by comparing himself with his contemporaries. He had always sought the reassurance of being liked and respected so as to minimise the stigma of his career. Elstow however had not yet been touched by the revivial of spiritual faith that was sweeping the country in the wake of the new Puritan preachers. In places it reached fever pitch, new Messiahs claimed to be the embodiment of the returned Christ and strange sects began to proliferate. In Bedford itself, the stirrings of the revival had begun. One afternoon when John had finished work, he decided to do a little window shopping. It was a warm summer's day and people were in a cheerful mood. He was greeted by many with whom he was acquainted through his work and he felt warmed by their affection. He passed the time of day with one but then became interested in a conversation he overheard amongst some women.

The women were sitting outside their houses, lace-making and cleaning some brassware. One elderly woman was too frail to work, but she was certainly able to contribute to the discussion.

'I don't believe I've ever known anything like it,' she was saying. 'The Spirit of God is really in Pastor Gifford for sure, the services are so full of God's presence. How I wish I was twenty years younger and I had this whole revival to look forward to.'

John went over to the group and greeted them.

'God bless you,' they replied, almost in unison.

'I couldn't help overhearing,' John went on. 'Which church do you attend?'

'Bedford Church, young man,' the old woman replied. 'Pastor Gifford's church. You should come. Are you local?'

'From Elstow.'

'Oh, well then, do come, you'll see the greatest outpouring of God's spirit you've ever known. God's grace is so wonderful that he should think to bless us so greatly, we, who have sinned so much.'

Then another woman spoke, hardly able to contain her enthusiasm. 'Since I've been going I've really understood how Satan can divert your thoughts from the truth. How he can make you think that you are good and successful in your good works and yet Pastor Gifford teaches us rightly, that all man's goodness is as filthy rags before God. I've learnt to trust God for my salvation, for by his grace I am saved and I am at rest because I've been born again. It's wonderful.' She smiled at John with a true affection in her eyes. 'Do come, sir, and see for yourself. You will not regret it.'

John smiled in reply, uncertain. He was out of his depth. He had thought he understood religion, but the women were speaking in a new language and he did not understand it. They had said that man's good works were not enough to gain salvation. What then would ensure it? They were obviously certain of their salvation, but had they done nothing for it? Doubt gripped his heart, the afternoon grew cold and Bedford unfriendly.

He stood and raised his hat, promising the ladies that he would come to Bedford Church. He felt compelled to do so for if he could not gain his salvation through abstaining from swearing or dancing, then all his self-sacrifice was for nothing. He could not bear that thought. Doubting and uncertain, John started for home to persuade Mary to come to Pastor Gifford's Bedford Church.

He arrived in one of his desperate moods, unhappily denouncing Elstow parish church as a den of hypocrites with little understanding of the true nature of faith, and loudly declaring that he had learnt more of Christianity from the women on one afternoon than he had ever learned from the prating Anglicans.

Worship at Elstow Church was therefore impossible for the Bunyans, and Mary accompanied John to Bedford church, delighted at John's increased interest in spirituality though nervous as well about the extremes in his attitudes.

The walk to Bedford was not a short one, not nearly as easy as crossing the green to the parish church in Elstow, but when they arrived for the first time, she, herself, found a real welcome and some enthusiastic friends. John too, found sympathy and friendship at the small Puritan meeting place, especially from its pastor, John Gifford, who warmed to John and became his spiritual mentor.

John, still guilt ridden and uncomprehending, approached the reassuring figure of Pastor John Gifford. As they lunched together, or strolled in the country, John recounted tales of his sin, his swearing, his dancing and drinking and his evil mind. Gifford could sometimes hardly suppress a smile at John's tales of woe. John was convinced that he was the world's worst sinner and could not be comforted, not even by Gifford's own colourful history and misspent youth which far outstripped his own in its misdemeanours.

Gifford had been a Royalist in the Civil War, a major. He was born and brought up in Kent. In 1648 the last spasm of the Civil War took place. The King was in captivity, Parliament desperately trying to negotiate a constitutional monarchy with him, but he would have none of it. In Kent an uprising occurred and led by the Earl of Norwich twelve thousand men – Gifford among them – began to march on London to rescue the King. The arrogant army was well trained and convinced of the rightness of their cause; they saw this as their last chance to restore the monarchy. Parliament, however, was not unprepared and they sent one of their greatest military leaders, General Fairfax, to head the assault against the Royalist rebellion. This was to be a bloody denouement to a bitter war. The two armies met in Maidstone and turned the town into a battleground. Civilians found their houses taken over, their homes bombarded by cannon shot and their streets turned into a stage set for vicious hand-to-hand fighting. The stakes were high and many men were wounded and killed, but the agony was short. Out of the twelve thousand who had marched with the Earl of Norwich fourteen hundred surrendered. The rest were either dead, or escaped. Amongst those captured was the notorious John Gifford, who, at this time, was not the pious man he was to become. He had a vindictive nature and a vicious and sadistic reputation and consequently was not released with most of the other soldiers, all of whom were sent home. Gifford and ten others were condemned to hang.

Gifford lay in prison to await his death, still with no thought of repentance even though the gates of hell were just a few hours away. The night before his execution his sister came to pay him one last visit. Whether by a miracle (as the Bedford congregation believed) or by fate she discovered that the guards were asleep and the doors open. Gifford needed little persuasion to take the opportunity to escape. His sister left him to his own devices and he found a hiding place in a nearby field. He crept into the bottom of a ditch and stayed there, cold, damp and extremely uncomfortable for three days.

Once the hue and cry had died down he travelled to London in disguise, eventually reaching Bedford, where he settled down. He pretended to be a doctor and practised medicine, with some success, for a number of months. He made his presence felt in Bedford, drinking, whoring and, in particular, gambling. Like most drunken gamblers of his ilk, he was not a good loser. As he watched his money cross the table, he would grow violently angry. One night he suffered a particularly heavy loss and raged and swore his way home, promising himself that he would never gamble again. It is unlikely that he would have kept that promise had he not come across a religious book, written by a Mr Bolton. He idly opened the book and something in it convinced him of his failures. Like John Bunyan, that night he learned the meaning of guilt and suffered greatly in recollection of his previous actions. He was noticeably subdued for a month. He suffered, if for a shorter time, the uncertainty of his soul's eternal state that John anguished over for years. After a month, he came to the realisation of God's forgiveness for man's sins through Christ.

It was not easy for him to convince his fellows that such a

change had taken place; unlike Saul who became St Paul, he had no miracles to demonstrate his authenticity. But he had obviously some ability at persuasion, having posed success-fully as a doctor for some time. Moreover, how he escaped the execution of his sentence is not clear, but escape he did. Perhaps that was miracle enough and for the last five years of his life, during which he became pastor of Bedford Church, he dedicated himself to the Puritan faith. He never lost sight of the demands that the holiness of God placed upon him.

It was this man who preached to the searching John, who was still convinced of his own inadequacy. The holiness that the others in the congregation exhibited was a genuineness of heart that John sensed he did not have. His religion was still external, he still doubted and mistrusted God. He did not understand, nor could he feel the great forgiveness that these people witnessed to.

Nevertheless, the change continued to take place in John's outward life and its effects grew deeper and more demanding. Already he had started to break with his old ways, and he soon began to turn from some of the bad company he kept. His friendship with Harry was broken. John had grown pious and the rift was a source of bitterness between them. At first John had begun to correct his friend's language and he had tried to persuade him to join in the spiritual revival that was touching Bedford. Harry, though, was of a more philosophical turn of mind and he was not bowed by feelings of guilt, nor was he convinced by the stories of hell and eternal damnation. Harry was too interested in the life he was living to worry about any future one, so he would not risk self-sacrifice for nothing. He found John's new piety irritating, especially when he tried to proselytise and he soon told John that he did not want to know.

They had not seen each other for several months when they met on the road between Elstow and Bedford. John still did not want to lose the friendship completely, nor did he want it to end so sadly, so he greeted Harry in the hope of repairing the damage.

'Hello,' returned Harry cautiously.

'How are you?' John asked.

Harry replied that he was feeling **** great.

John sighed. His friend had not changed at all, and it puzzled him that he did not suffer the conviction of guilt that he, himself, felt so strongly. He felt a twinge of envy at Harry's carefree manner. 'Harry,' he reproached. 'Why do you swear so much? Aren't you in the least bit afraid of what will become of your soul? What if you should die in this condition?'

Harry was not pleased by this question. His worst fears about John were now confirmed. Moreover the threat of hell had far greater potency then and it was an act of genuine courage to defy the ultimate fate of the soul. He replied wittily enough, 'What would the Devil do for company, if it weren't for the likes of me?' Among the many converts that John was to make in the future, Harry was not likely to be one.

Despite his awkward good intentions, John had still not fully resolved the questioning within himself and was still vulnerable to the teachings of many groups that had come into being as a result of the new religious tolerance. Some of these groups were accepted by the Puritans, and others were not, but the atmosphere was such that many cults were able to survive. John in his questioning frame of mind came across one such group, the Ranters.

As their name suggests they were unorthodox and not highly thought of by most of their contemporaries. Their teaching, even today, would be extreme, and then it was beyond heresy! They held that the Lord had forgiven, through Christ, all sin: past, present and future. Christ had died to save man from sin and from the Law. Therefore once people had committed themselves to belief in Christ they were forgiven and could therefore sin, in the knowledge of their forgiveness. How could someone who was assured of salvation commit a wrong large enough to negate that salvation? This approach had its attractions for John. He was convinced that he could never stop sinning and could never please God with his actions. Like Luther before him he felt his inadequacy keenly. On reading the literature of the Ranters, he was attracted by the thought that whatever he did he was forgiven, and thus assured of a place in heaven.

However his initial interest was short-lived. John soon shied away from the Ranters when he saw again the old man who had first begun to reveal the scriptures to him. This man had become a Ranter. He claimed that he had searched through all religions and had now discovered the true way. When John saw this doctrine in practice in this man, he was horrified. The man was entirely carefree and careless, given over to every whim and fancy. He used his forgiveness as an excuse to do anything. John was reminded of his father and the speed with which he married his new young wife. The old man mocked faithful Christianity. John could not reconcile the practice of the Ranters with their apparently attractive theology; sadly he dropped the idea of becoming a Ranter. It could not be that easy, and yet still he did not know which way he should turn to assure himself of salvation.

5

INNER TURMOIL

John continued to attend the Bedford church but, despite the welcome that he and Mary had received, what he saw was so alien to him that he could not feel part of it. Here was a congregation of people utterly bound up in the love of God. Not one of them seemed to doubt that salvation was theirs. Not one of them seemed to have any difficulty in living the life of holiness that was required of them. John longed for certainty. He yearned for someone to say to him, 'You are saved, your name is in the Book of Life, be assured you have done enough,' but no one said that – at least, no one he felt he could believe. He had to have proof, proof that his faith was enough.

It was that word 'faith' which confused him. In the Bible, to which he had retreated after his brush with the Ranters, he discovered this verse: 'To one is given by the Spirit the word of wisdom, to another the word of knowledge by the same Spirit and to another faith.' (1 Corinthians 12: 8–9) 'Faith' seemed such an inexact word. What were its outward signs? How did you know if you had faith? If faith did have outward signs (for instance the ability to move a mountain), John felt convinced of his lack of faith. Was he then to be damned?

However depressed he got about his ultimate fate, John could never quite believe that he was damned for ever without the hope of rescue. Other people, after all, including his own wife, were assured of their rescue. John delved deeper and deeper into the nature of faith and his own soul.

Much of his agonising occurred when he wandered from place to place, mending and collecting. On his back he carried the tools of his trade, in his mind he carried his doubts. He walked miles in those months of spiritual conflict and much of his inward debate was conducted on the roads around Elstow and Bedford.

He concluded on one of these walks that in order to have proof he must force God's hand. Only a miracle would prove his salvation was assured. There had been a shower of rain earlier that day and the rutted path was full of puddles. John was reminded of the story of Gideon who put out a fleece for God to prove to him His will. Gideon asked God to make the fleece wet with dew and the ground dry and then the following night he had reversed the sign and asked for the ground to be wet and the fleece untouched by the dew. John believed that God had met Gideon's request and performed the miracle because Gideon's faith was sufficient to cause the miracle. If Gideon could do it then why couldn't he, John, do the same? Or at least something similar. 'If I just have the faith, I can make the ruts where the water is dry and the surrounding ground wet.' He wanted to lift the water out of the ruts and spread it at his feet. It was a simple enough miracle, small enough for a man with faith the size of a mustard seed. If it worked it would prove once and for all that John had his faith and was saved.

He took a deep breath and opened his mouth to command the puddles to obey him, but then a thought struck him: what if he were not in the right spiritual state? He should pray first and thus assure himself of his own purity before he attempted his miracle. If he were to try it without a pure mind the results might not mean anything.

John put down his tools and knelt beneath the hedge at the side of the road. He prayed hard for a while and then turned back towards the puddles, but another thought now pestered him: if he could not do the miracle now, what would that mean? If his mind was pure but his faith could not respond, did that mean that he had no faith and therefore no hope of salvation? He decided to pray for a bit longer, to make sure that he had the power of faith. He stayed by the side of the road for some time wondering whether he had the faith to

perform the miracle and trying to pluck up the courage to
test that faith, all the time terrified that he would fail and be
sure once and for all that he was damned. At last, uncertain
and very afraid, prompted by the darkening sky, John went
his way still unresolved.

John, the man of dreams and nightmares, dreamed that
night. His doubt and fear was such a contrast to the
happiness and assurance of the congregation at Bedford that
he saw it represented in a dream. There they were, the people
of his congregation, sitting on the sunny side of a mountain.
They were laughing and resting in the warm sun and yet he,
John, was cold and frightened, separated from the warmth
of the sun by a huge wall. He shivered in the snow and frost.
He was surrounded by dark storm clouds that threatened
him and between him and the people who were so happy
stood the wall. There was no way round it or over it or under
it. He longed to escape the cold and find a way through. If he
could just get through that wall then he too would enjoy
warmth and peace. He searched up and down in his strange
dream seeking the way until at last he came to a narrow gap,
like a little doorway. He tried to scramble through it, but it
was too straight and narrow, for he was a big and stocky
man. Nevertheless he would not be beaten, and as a baby
struggles through the birth canal, so John persisted through
the gap and at last he got his head through. He could now
feel the warmth of the sun on his face, and it seemed to give
him strength. He twisted round and turned until his
shoulders burst through; once that far it needed only one last
heave to get him through entirely. Finally he was in the
sunlight, able to share with his fellow Christians the warmth
of the sun. He had been born again.

John explained the dream later as meaning that the
mountain was the Church of the Living God and the sun was
God's face throwing down warming beams. The wall was the
Word of God and the gap, Jesus Christ, who is the Way. It
was a narrow gap, for only those who truly wanted to get
through it would succeed.

At that moment though, John was not yet through the

gap, or at least he did not think so. Doubts still came rattling into his heart like the clatter of hooves. Whereas some Bible verses encouraged him, others utterly demoralised him. 'For it [salvation] is not of man that willeth, nor of him that runneth, but of the God that sheweth mercy' (Romans 9: 16). What if God did not want to show mercy to him? How did he know if he was chosen? No matter how much he wanted to be chosen, or how hard he worked to prove his worth, if God had not chosen him then that was that. Once again John was tempted to give it all up and go back to a life of indifference, for he felt now as he had felt that day on the village green; he was damned and should therefore enjoy life while he could.

By this time John was making himself ill with worry; sometimes all he wanted to do was to sink and die. At least then he would find the answer. Let hell claim him. Surely the certainty of his damnation would be better than the uncertainty of his salvation.

At last, in the depths of his misery, a shaft of light shot through. In a comforting audible voice someone spoke to him in his mind and said, 'Look at the generations of old and see did ever any trust in the Lord and was confounded?'

John grasped at the voice and its hope and clung to it with the desperation of a shipwrecked man who clings to a plank, hoping that it can save his life but not sure that it will. Just as John could not quite believe he was damned, he could never quite believe that he was saved. He hunted through the Bible, trying to find an example of someone who had trusted in God and been betrayed. The search went on for a year: the whole Bible spoke of God's faithfulness towards those who trusted Him, and John was encouraged. His anxiety lifted a little, life was improving, work was good, Mary was healthily pregnant, God appeared to be blessing him. God must be pleased with John Bunyan. But John's imagination was still his enemy and it plagued him with the nightmares of his childhood. He persistently swung from one view to the other, sometimes saved, sometimes damned.

It was not over yet.

'Simon! Simon! Satan desires to have you! Simon!

Simon!' The old torment had begun again. Voices in the
night. John peered into the darkness trying to see the man
who had called to him. He looked to the crest of the hill
running parallel to the lane. In the twilight he could just see
the shrubs and hedges that stuck up like a coxcomb on the
line of the hill; he could see no one and yet the voice, the
shout, had been so clear. Nervously John turned back to the
lane. He shifted the burden on his back, readjusted his tools
and began to walk on, keen to reach home before it became
pitch black. He could only hear the sound of his own
footsteps; none followed after. He seemed to be alone and
yet he was sure he was being followed. The back of his neck
prickled and he tried to dare himself to look behind. 'Simon!
Simon!' the voice said again, this time at his shoulder. John
gasped, almost screamed, and turned suddenly on his
assailant – but there was no one there. The voice, though,
went on, 'Satan wants you'. The torture was too great. John
began to run, desperate to get as far from that place as he
could. Despite the weight of his tools he found the strength
to pound up the lane with speed. The anvil on his back
bounced against his spine, making him catch his breath and
groan. He dropped a small hammer and struggled to pick it
up quickly. He looked in fear at the road behind him; feeling
someone close, someone evil, threatening. He gripped the
hammer at his side, not bothering to try to replace it in its
tool bag. The voice called him once more, making him
respond with a cry of 'No!' He was growing breathless, his
legs weakened beneath him and he knew if he stopped now,
he would not be able to start again. At last his cottage came
into view and he found the strength to sprint towards the
light and safety, safety from the pursuing hound of hell.

John staggered into his home, terrified and out of breath.
He hoped desperately that no one had seen him running who
might spread the story in the village of how John Bunyan ran
helter skelter through the streets like a madman. Mary had
grown used to his moods but the village had not.

Terror was a new aspect of John's uncertainty. Mary
listened to his story and soothed him but she was unsure

what to make of it. Could it be true? Had her husband been pursued by the very Devil himself down the streets of Elstow? Or did he suffer a disease of the mind? Was he going mad? She saw little to reassure herself in either explanation and John, although calmer now, was still sufficiently alarmed to bolt the doors and close the windows. He was convinced the Devil was torturing him in an effort to get his soul, and he blamed himself for being vulnerable to temptation, an easy target. It was his own sin that attracted the demons to him. He was, in a way, an accessory to his own damnation, either that or he was possessed. Like a child carried away by gypsies he struggled and protested but he could not break free.

John called to God in his pain, he begged Christ to speak to him for he still longed for certainty, for a tangible sign that would give him peace of mind about his salvation. He demanded material knowledge of the Kingdom of God; like Thomas he wanted to put his fist into the wounds in the side of the risen Christ. He repeated his troubles again and again to Gifford and the congregation. Gifford tried to assure him of God's love, but John was no easy convert, not through any hostility to God, but through his implacable hostility to himself. He read that the wicked never rest, that they are tossed on a tumultuous sea. Surely, he reasoned, he must have committed the greatest sin, the sin against the Holy Spirit, that sin which could not be forgiven. He must have ultimately forfeited his salvation, otherwise God would have rescued him by now. Why else did God ignore him? Why else did Christ never answer his call? He must have offended God. He must be abhorrent in the sight of God.

But still John prayed. He begged God to be kind to him; perhaps He could be persuaded by the sheer force of John's persistence to love him. John knelt in his room alone, his wife at work in the house, lonely and helpless in the face of her husband's misery. John rocked himself in the depths of despair, crying, moaning, still pleading with God for forgiveness, but more importantly for the proof of that forgiveness, for the certainty of salvation that he saw in his fellow Christians. The room was cold and lonely and there was no vision of Christ to comfort him, just a gentle tugging at his coat. John froze. What did that mean – that tugging like a kitten playing with his coat tails? John began to shiver, the smell of sulphur was in his nostrils. The tugging jerked and jangled his every nerve. The Devil was at his shoulder, in the house! 'Bow down and worship me,' he hissed, tempting the terrified man.

John was distracted from his prayers. He was a fool to be so easily drawn away, he was so faithless that he could not even repudiate the Devil in his own home. 'You are very hot for mercy,' said the Devil sarcastically. 'But I will cool you, I will cool you though you be seven years in the chilling of your heart.' The whisper was real, the threat potent, the very incarnation of evil was tormenting the man in his room, alone. 'I will have my end accomplished,' the tugging went on pulling, pulling, pulling.

John was sweating, he seemed to be suffocating, there was no air in the room and yet he was shaking with cold. He gathered up his courage and his faith to send the Devil hurtling. 'No!' he cried, and his voice shook the house. Mary hovering uncertainly in the next room was terrified, afraid of disturbing her husband's prayer, but anguished by his pain. John collapsed on the floor, sobbing, begging for death, for it seemed to him that the longer he lived the more chance the Devil had of gaining his eternal soul. He lay on the floor shaking and sick, exhausted by his mania; if now there was a chance that he was holy enough to go to heaven, then surely a merciful God would take him. If he lived another moment longer, the Devil might win him back and divide him for ever from God.

John swung deeper and deeper into despair and depression; sometimes he would grasp at the Light, but on the whole he sunk down into the abyss of darkness. He would discover the comfort of salvation only briefly before the threatening voice came again. 'Sell Christ!' it said now, 'Sell him!' time and time again. Could he resist in his own strength? Was he a strong enough Christian to hold on to

Christ? 'Sell him! Sell him!' How could he resist? This persistent voice, this endless fear – would it end if he did as was suggested? Would the attack abate? Would there be at least peace from the voice, if not from his conscience? Anything would be better than the ever-pestering voice of Satan. If he submitted to the Devil then at least he would be left alone. John let go, exhausted. In his mind he gave up Christ for the Devil and fell into despair.

John was close to a complete breakdown. His work gave him no comfort for it seemed to him a further indication of his inadequacy. He had not been able to improve himself and did not prosper as he felt the good man should. He spoke openly of his fears to another member of the congregation who offered him no help and instead believed all that John said of himself. John's battle was a long and severe one, but it was to end far more abruptly than it had begun.

He had become familiar with his moods and his depression and he indulged them and fed on them. He was ruled by self-pity and self-effacement and Mary, however hard she tried, could not lift him out of it. Night after night he was to seek escape in his moods, sometimes out at the inn, sometimes alone in the house with Mary. He would sit by the fire and brood, waiting for revelation. He watched the flames, lonely and convinced that this conflict would never cease. His wife sat opposite him quietly sewing, relieved that at least tonight he was with her and not pouring out his heart alone in their room. She watched the misery on her husband's face, lit by the fire and she too wondered if this desperate search, this awful black mood was going to end in anything other than disaster. Suddenly as she watched she saw a flame flicker in his eyes. What was it? He sat up and looked at her, excited.

'Mary,' he said, 'is there a verse which says I should go to Jesus?'

'I don't know,' she replied. 'I don't think I know what you mean.' She kept silent, fearing another outburst of hope followed by the inevitable despair.

Something had stirred in John's memory. 'See that ye

refuse him not that speaketh,' (Hebrews 12: 25) was a verse
he had come across in his earlier searching, but he had not
understood it. It had echoed through his struggles. 'Should
go to Jesus. And to an innumerable company of angels.'
(Hebrews 12: 22–24).

'Oh now I know, I know!' exclaimed John. He had seen
the call in the verses. At last he had seen the 'Light' like Paul
had on the Damascus road all those years ago. For John it
was just as dramatic. He did not have to do anything, he was
or would be accepted by God, just as he was. However sinful,
desperate, neurotic and wicked, God would take him and
keep him if he would only ask Him to. All God asked was
that he come forward as he was. There was no test of holiness
to pass, no standards to reach, all he had to be was willing.
Salvation was a gift that he needed only to accept.

That night revelation led John across the divide. He
finally struggled through the gap in the wall to the warm side
of the mountain. Almost two years of struggle had ended.
John, with sudden ease, had found the way out of the prison
of the Giant Despair.

6

FAMILY AND CALLING

Although John had shed the years of neuroticism and left his dark moods behind him, it was a long time before Mary believed in his new-found stability. She had grown used to staggering from one crisis to the next and still expected John to swing wildly back into misery. As a result she became stoically self-sufficient, she did not trust him.

It was while he was still suffering his deep depression that their first child was born and it was in this mood of self-reliance forced upon her by her husband's demons that Mary faced the birth of their child. Like so many fathers before and after him, John had waited anxiously while his first child was born. His wife's pregnancy and labour seemed only to expose his own inadequacies and he waited and worried. At last there was the sound of a child's cries and they shared (at least momentarily) the joy of the birth of an active healthy daughter.

Whether they discovered it then, or whether it was a little while later when John noticed their tiny baby, Mary, fumbling in front of her, or saw that she was unaware of the objects he danced before her eyes, her blind eyes, is not known. John says nothing of the discovery but sometimes, in his worst moments of self-doubt, he thought Mary was being punished for his lack of faith.

The crisis of doubt past, John found his faith and began to grow. Little Mary had become a part of their married lives and she was a joy, not a burden, to the young parents, though John must have wondered with trepidation what kind of life was to befall his blind daughter, whom he loved so dearly. John began to feel confident of God's love, of his

ability and willingness to see them through. As the months
passed Mary too came to believe in her husband's more
settled state of mind. She felt, for the first time, that she
could really relax in his presence. Even so, it was with
apprehension that the couple approached the birth of their
second child, Elizabeth. John had come to understand God's
love, but he still feared the punishment of his dreams and it
was with great relief that he saw their second baby girl was
born perfect.

The Bunyans' prosperity increased, and encouraged by
their success, they moved into Bedford to be nearer the
church and better business. The move itself was a pleasing
indication of their increased respectability and prosperity,
but no sooner was the move completed than John became ill.
Doubtless the mental turmoil of the previous few years had
taken its toll. Whatever the reason, John was ill enough to
believe he was going to die and as he grew weaker some of the
old conflicts returned. The fear of hell, the sound of the
tormented, rang in his ears and he again began to doubt
God's mercy. But John was now a more rational man and he
realised quickly enough that the state of his body was
affecting his state of mind. He hung on to his belief in
salvation and the illness passed.

The years in Bedford went by peacefully enough after that.
John's wife nursed him through a winter of illness and then
she had two more children, both boys. The act of child-
bearing was not only more frequent in those days but more
hazardous and often weakening. She was strained by the
constant effort of chasing after young Mary and trying to
equip her for the life of darkness that she led. Her condition
deteriorated so much that she became prey to some infection
or perhaps she was congenitally ill but she rapidly lost
strength and died. They had been married only ten years and
John was not yet thirty.

Little Mary can have been little more than seven or eight
years old, while the others had barely left their mother's
breast. John came to understand a little better why his father
had remarried so quickly on the death of his mother. The

congregation of the Bedford Church rallied round; John was becoming a well-loved figure and he excelled in his work, the people willingly comforted him. He had always felt everything strongly and his sense of loss was no less keen. He worked day and night to keep the family and tried to set a little time aside to play with his children.

He lost too that early mentor of spiritual life, John Gifford. There was no longer the humorous man's sharp tongue and perceptive preaching to act as a foil to John's intellect, just as there was no more laughter in his house to calm his soul since Mary had gone. In the church a new pastor was appointed, a rather frail man called John Burton; he was no substitute for Gifford and John found himself more alone in his spiritual life than he had ever been. Moreover, it was now 1657 and while Bedford Church's new pastor tried to establish the church as a going concern, instituting the keeping of records, the political climate looked ever more threatening. By this time there were strong indications that the English Republic had feet of clay.

On January 8th Whitehall Palace was set on fire in an attempt to murder Cromwell. The attempt failed but unrest in the country was now obvious; the austerity of the Puritan era was over-severe and it awakened Royalist tendencies in men and women who would not otherwise have cared either way. They wanted life to be a bit more fun. Cromwell, shaken by this attempt and growing old, began to entertain thoughts of becoming king. Bedford, alarmed by this tendency, sent 'The Humble and Serious Testimony' up to Parliament. This was a petition to Cromwell to refuse the Crown and it was signed, among others, by some members of the church at Bedford. John did not sign the petition for, despite the success of 'The Humble and Serious Testimony', such acts were becoming dangerous; John had four young children to look after and within him a growing ability to preach, a talent that he did not want to jeopardise.

John's gift for preaching had come as a surprise to him, but he had found he was an eloquent speaker. People appreciated and understood what he said. Conscientious as always, he decided that it was his responsibility to use this gift. After the birth of his blind daughter and the death of Mary, he could claim to understand a little of the suffering some people had undergone. He was a sympathetic listener and a most convinced convert. Just in the way that he had once profoundly doubted God's love towards man, he now fervently believed it and channelled the energy that had once been sublimated in dancing and bell-ringing and then into depression into his preaching. All the spare time he had was dedicated to bringing the salvation he received within the reach of those who, as yet, did not understand its nature.

He preached with urgency, not just because he wanted to save people before they died (for he was, to begin with, a 'Fire and Brimstone' preacher, who feared that his subjects would very soon burn in hell) but because he could see that the Puritan age was in its twilight and soon the darkness of another monarchy would deny him his freedom to preach and save. Nevertheless he had time enough to learn a great deal about the nature of oratory and preaching.

He began by terrifying his congregation into heaven, or rather out of hell. He used the images that had been so real to him in his youth of hell, the Devil and eternal torment. He described God who punished and condemned those who did not follow Him. But as he grew in the knowledge of his faith and observed the lives of his brothers and sisters in Christ and experienced God's love in his own life he began to modify the way he preached. John had come to know the positive influences of God's love and grace. He was no longer a Christian by fear or guilt, but because he understood that God loved him. 'I altered my preaching,' he says. 'I still preached what I saw and felt, but now I worked to hold faith in Jesus and his relationship and benefit to the world.' He emphasised now that the remission of sins through Jesus Christ by faith was to be greeted with joy and he worded his readings and illustrations by examples from the saints.

John, the man of insecurities, ever conscious of his evil self, found that he was assaulted by temptations. Sometimes when he was preaching, he was tempted to burst out with a stream of obscenities just to see the reaction. This, he says, was Satan tempting him to misuse his power as an orator; sometimes the Devil came in the form of a heckler in the crowd, shouting at him and abusing him. Sometimes John revelled in his ability to manipulate the crowd and enjoyed, with pride, the verbal fencing with his hecklers. He knew he must guard against this too; the Devil now came to him subtly but just as dangerously as before.

He was not, however, constantly fighting these temptations. He could get so involved with the task of saving souls that he would almost faint from the effort of trying to make them see; sometimes he would be burdened for one particular person and he would plead with that person to enter the Kingdom. When he saw one turn away he would almost weep for their loss; the loss of one stranger in a vast kingdom could move him more than his own hardships.

His reputation began to grow, his powerful echoing voice reverberated in the county. With his red hair and striking features, he could stand out in a crowd without raising his voice to preach, and once he did preach, his charisma was magnetic. He spoke with the conviction of one who had much for which to thank God and who had a total assurance of God's existence and love. Gone was the doubter, gone was the anguish of a man obsessed by his own failings. All this was replaced by the confidence of a man at peace with himself and the world. He missed Mary, of course, but an older, more mature John now took on the responsibilities of a father.

The acclaim that he had once looked for and despaired of was now his and, for the moment at least, the stigma of being a tinker did not matter. He was even strong enough to face, amidst the mockery of the growing crowds of Royalists, the first hints of opposition.

7

GATHERING CLOUDS

A typical venue for a preaching engagement was the village market place. John and his team would set up on a reasonably quiet pitch and begin attracting the attention of the busy marketgoers. John would stand on a box or a bale of hay, sometimes on the back of a cart, and make himself known. It was no easy task to draw the farmers and the villagers away from their main business of buying and selling their goods and bartering for the best prices. First of all, John's colleagues would mix among the crowd, telling everyone the preaching was about to begin and couldn't be missed because it concerned the welfare of their souls. Once a small group of people had gathered, expressing a passing interest, John would begin and was quickly in his element. His strong healthy voice boomed out across the market, competing with the calling of the market stallholders. Not that he was the only one proclaiming a message, for this was a time of free thought and free expression and there were other cults and sects who had much to gain in humiliating the opposition.

It was one afternoon when things were going quite well that John found his flow of speech interrupted. 'John Bunyan!' a woman's voice called from the crowd. 'Why don't you dispense with the Bible and let the Spirit guide your speech?' John looked fondly at the battered and faithful Bible to which he was constantly referring. He laughed and replied quickly, 'No! For then the Devil would be too strong for me.' The crowd laughed and murmured in agreement. Anne Blackley, the woman who had challenged John, had no support from this crowd for her cause. She tried again, but at last the 'hushes' and threats of the crowd drove her away.

Anne Blackley's words disturbed John, for she was a Quaker. John was apprehensive of the Quakers, as they seemed to him to espouse a theology dangerously close to that of the Ranters. They claimed that man could interpret the Bible according to his inner light which God would guide. There was no need for any restrictions to be placed on a man's thoughts except that which the Spirit could be trusted to provide. 'But how,' thought John, 'did you discern God's Spirit except through the Bible and learning?' The Quakers claimed, too, that Jesus was a man whose divinity was as much to do with their recollection and worship of him, as what he had shown to be divine on earth. His spirit was resurrected in his people. John took this to mean that the Quakers had thrown away the Bible and denied the resurrection of Christ, replacing this doctrine with a dangerous mysticism. The Quakers were John's *bête noire*; he opposed them violently and Anne Blackley's heckling only confirmed his worst opinions of them.

In essence, however, there was not such a great difference as John believed between the Quakers and himself. They were still formulating their theories, and perhaps in that process their behaviour and beliefs sometimes veered into the extreme. They were tolerated by the regime of the time, for Cromwell took no action against them, but they suffered persecution and abuse from their contemporaries. John, although never violent, in some ways fuelled the fire of these attackers and his first published work consisted of an attack on the Quakers.

In order to guide people away from what he saw as this dangerous threat to human salvation, he wrote and published *Some Vindications of Gospel Truths*. He was answered by a young Quaker of twenty-three, Edward Burrough, who had heard John preach. He accused John of being a 'hireling', a professional minister, a man who preached for money and not for the salvation of souls. John, incensed by this accusation, replied that Burrough was 'a

grossly railing Rabshekah' and he wrote a second treatise,
Some More Vindications of Gospel Truths.

After that John's publishing career was assured as was his
notoriety. His condemning tone when he spoke of the
Quakers gave the impression that he was a stern and austere
man, intolerant of other believers. He was incautious with
regard to them, but this was not generally in character with
his more positive style of preaching, nor did its vehemence
last for long. Edward Burrough was to die at the age of
twenty-eight in Newgate prison and John himself was later
to witness the faith and piety of many Quakers. As a result he
came to believe that they were not, after all, the Devil's
children but a faithful misguided cult. He continued his
preaching and writing against the Quakers all his life, but as
he grew older and he shared their prison cells, his attitudes
mellowed.

John's debates were not just with Quakers. Depite the
religious freedom that existed under Cromwell, there were
still many who felt that only those trained, specifically
educated and ordained had a right to preach from the Word
of God. John did not have this education, they argued, and
so was prone to heresy. How could a man who knew no
Latin or Greek preach accurate doctrine? John himself,
when using a Latin phrase, was careful to say 'the Latin I
borrow'. Just as John feared the Quakers, many people
feared him. It seemed to them that he made dangerously free
with the gospels.

He was now sufficiently well known to cause interest
wherever he went, and it was a common thing for him to be
stopped in the street or in an inn. On one such occasion, on
the way to Cambridge, when he had paused on the journey
for a drink, a university man recognised him and began to
question him.

'How can you claim a right to preach,' began the man, 'if
you haven't read the Bible in Latin? How do you know that
your English translation is a true copy of the original?'

John smiled. He had grown used to these sudden attacks
and his quick wit was a part of his fame. 'Ah,' he said,

feigning shock and enthusiastic surprise. 'I take it that you must be the man who owns the one original copy of the Bible, the one from which all other copies and translations are made.'

The man coughed in an embarrassed manner, already spotting his coming downfall. 'No,' he replied, 'but I believe mine to be a true copy.'

John chuckled and turned to go. 'Well, I believe mine to be a true copy also.'

When the weather was inclement for the market place, or it was the occasion of Sunday worship, a barn or a local hall or someone's home would be John's church. His intention to preach was often advertised locally, so both supporters and opponents would be aware of his movements. Frequently, a service would be interrupted by a heckler, but not all of these were local yobs after a fight and some trouble. Some came to defeat the 'prating tinker' with intellectual argument. One such man was Professor Thomas Smith, Rector of Gawcat, Cambridge, Professor of Arabic and a reader in Rhetoric at Christ's College. Thomas regarded it as his holy duty to challenge John just as John regarded it as his sacred duty to defy both the Quakers and the Anglicans. Smith feared that John would pervert Christianity and damn many innocent souls to hell.

On this occasion John preached his usual sermon, calling the people to repent and accept salvation. All the people in those days were baptised at birth and therefore were considered by the established Church already to be believers and saved from sin.

Smith rose and interrupted John, hardly able to control his anger. 'You sir, Bunyan! Why do you call the people to repent, when the Anglican Church has already saved them from their sins by infant baptism? Paul wrote in his letters to believers, why then do you preach from such a letter if no one here is a Christian? You offend us, sir, you're not fit to preach.'

The people who filled the barn watched and waited while John summoned his reply. It would certainly be useful to them were the professor to prove his case, for it would release them from the need to take John seriously.

John, however, countered the attack. 'Jesus did not compliment his listeners all the time. Was he unfit to preach?'

'How shall they preach except they are sent?' Smith boomed out across the barn.

'The church at Bedford sent me,' said John quietly.

Smith laughed at this. 'The church at Bedford sent you!' he mocked. 'That church is made up of nothing but lay people, there is no one there qualified to commission a minister. How can they choose a tinker to minister to them, to us!' Smith stormed out before John had a chance to reply, and a few people in the congregation followed him.

Smith did not leave it there though. Motivated by a genuine fear that John was preaching heresy, he published his concern in the form of an appeal to the people of Taft, four miles from the barn where John had preached that day. He set out his arguments against John, finishing his paper with an emotive appeal.

And now, sir, let me beseech you for God's sake, for your reputation's sake, for your children's sake, for your country's sake, for your immortal soul's sake to consider these things sadly and seriously, not think a tinker more infallible than the pure spouse of Christ, and foresee what will be the sad consequences.

Apparently John did not reply to this open letter, but someone else did. Henry Denne, himself a Cambridge man who believed in John's right to preach, wrote, 'You seem angry with the tinker because he strives to mend men's souls as well as kettles and pans.'

John had grown confident and was at peace with himself. He felt strong enough to face the weapons that the opposition would use. As he had become well known, William Dell of Yelden, the great preacher of the New Model Army, invited him to preach in his church. Undoubtedly

John as a young soldier had heard of this minister's ability, if not heard him preach himself, and now at the invitation of this great man John was to preach from his pulpit.

That day, like every other time, John preached with his heart burning to save every soul. He suffered as if he himself had given birth to each, but his talent and reputation were not wholly respected at Yelden. Dell had fought a long hard battle with his congregation to invite John; preaching in a barn or a market place was one thing, but on sanctified ground? From a pulpit? There had been strong opposition to his invitation and this was not helped by John implying that many had not yet realised God's salvation. A few took offence that they were being preached to by someone who was not ordained, a common tinker, and some did not attend. Perhaps it was a miscalculation on the part of Dell to invite the young man to preach at Yelden, for the darkening Puritan sky grew more threatening for John after that day.

8

THE BEGINNING OF REPRESSION

On May 29th, 1660 the inevitable happened; Charles II came to the British throne. Charles' opinions on religion were ambiguous to say the least. It appears that he converted to Roman Catholicism only on his deathbed, but it was thought that his sympathies were always with the Roman Catholics, a fact that discomforted the newly liberated Anglican clergy. It is safe to say that he had little affection for the Puritans who murdered his father, but in spite of that he did not allow the vengeful backlash on the general population which might have been expected. In the past, monarchs had persecuted their opposition almost to extinction, but in this case only the Regicides (those who signed the King's death warrant) were hunted and punished by execution. Two of the Regicides came from Bedford and both left the country. One, Sir Michael Livesey, seems to have escaped, for he was never heard of again; but a certain Colonel Okey was captured and hung, drawn and quartered.

It was clear to the Puritans and to John that their Golden Age was over. They could not yet be sure that Charles II had either the power or the desire to control the bitterness of his supporters. A dark apprehensive fear settled on the Puritans as the embittered Anglican clergy were reinstated and released from gaol. These men appealed to Charles to take steps to stamp out the heretics, but Charles did not really care; or rather, he wanted a tolerant society, a society which would allow minority groups to function, including (if not especially) the Catholics. He stated that any man could hold to his religious beliefs as long as they did not interfere with the peace of the realm; he intended to retain the throne a little longer than his inflexible father.

This liberal sentiment was not enough for the clergy. They feared not only another revolution through the tolerance of minority groups but also the rise of Catholicism and a return to the bosom of the Pope. Caught between those two possibilities and ruled by an indifferent King, the only hope for the clergy was recourse to earlier laws that had not been repealed by either Cromwell or the King. They reinstated the power of the parish priest and the Church. They reinstituted the Common Prayer Book and stated that only those who were licensed could preach, teach or lead worship, and then only with the help of the Prayer Book. Thus they returned the monopoly of religious worship to an élite, educated clergy and an inflexible ritual.

John, in the meantime, had met and married his second wife, Elizabeth. He was her first husband and she was more than ten years his junior. She was shortly to be faced with real adversity and would need all her youthful courage and energy. The Bedford Church had its premises confiscated and, perhaps as a result of the strain, John Burton, their second pastor, died. Against this gloomy and uncertain background, John continued to preach. He was famous throughout the county and had gained the nickname 'Bishop Bunyan', but for the makers of Restoration England he was infamous, a threat to the new conformity that the clergy so desperately wished to impose. Almost before the new restrictions had been brought into force the authorities began to hunt John. He had drawn attention to himself by preaching in William Dell's church and by battling so successfully with his intellectual opponents. It was not long since the executions of Archbishop Cranmer and Thomas More; the Law of England had changed little since then and those who challenged it could expect no mercy.

On November 12th, 1660, John was due to preach at a barn in Lower Samsell, about twelve miles from Bedford. On that cold day John set out, apprehensive but undeterred. Elizabeth watched him go. She was eight months pregnant and there was a rumour abroad that a warrant was out for

John's arrest, drawn up by Justice Francis Wingate who had
authority over a neighbouring jurisdiction; his function as a
Justice was that of a Magistrate, and he wanted to silence the
irritating preacher.

When John dismounted at Lower Samsell he was met by a
delegation of worried faces. A man took his horse but
instead of leading it away, he stood with it, expectant. One of
the delegation stepped forward; he was nervous, hunted-
looking. 'John, you must go back. Wingate has a warrant
out for you.'

John smiled reassuringly and patted the horse, signalling
the groom to lead it away. 'Thank you, brother, for your
concern, but I shall take the consequences of preaching.'

'But John...' the man protested urgently.

'No,' he said raising his finger to his lips to silence further
objections. He began to lead the way to the barn, placing his
hands on the shoulders of two of his would-be protectors. 'I
will not stir,' he went on. 'I must not, neither will I have the
meeting dismissed for this.' They were making their way
more positively towards the barn; already John's rhetoric
was working its spell on his friends. 'Our cause is good, we
need not be ashamed of it; to preach God's word is so good a
work that we shall be well rewarded for it.'

They made their way under the trees to the barn. John felt
his stomach tighten and his nerves quaver. He had shown
himself cheerful and courageous but he did not feel it. He
hung on to the thought of what his weaker or newly-
courageous brethren would think if he backed down now.
'But I was not as strong as I appeared,' he said later. If he ran
now, he would be safe, but a coward; and the movement
might collapse for want of someone to stand up to the
authorities. If he failed to face danger, what could he expect
of his congregations? His failure would strike fear into the
hearts of those who trusted him. He braced himself to take
the meeting.

He entered the barn, opened with prayer and began.
Immediately a constable and his companions burst in and
amidst the confusion the constable challenged him.

'John Bunyan! I must warn you that this meeting is illegal.'

John tried to go on but the constable and his two henchmen stepped forward and grabbed him. John bowed to the inevitable: he could not fight them, nor did he believe that he should try. He allowed himself to be led out, all the time shouting words of encouragement to those who watched, helpless and fearful.

'Don't be afraid,' he called back. 'It is a true blessing to suffer for Jesus' sake. We're not thieves or murderers. We know our cause is just.' He struggled against the constable to start one last sentence of reassurance. 'Our suffering is not justified. God will note it and bless us.' The constable and his men shouted him down and John went silently with them.

The arrest could not be followed through until the next day, as Justice Francis Wingate was away. John remained in the custody of a friend on his surety, spending the night at this man's home. He sent a message to his wife and waited in anxious anticipation for the following day.

Wingate dug up the 1535 Conventicle Act with which to indict John. The Act was over a hundred years old, instituted in the reign of Elizabeth I to protect the English Reformation from the Catholics. The Act stated that a man could not preach the gospel without first obtaining a licence, which he could only get through the Anglican authorities. Once caught, an offender would be given a three-month gaol sentence during which time he was given the opportunity to recant; if he did not, he was hanged.

John knew enough about the Act to realise he was in danger and Wingate delayed seeing him to keep John on tenterhooks. He was asked to remain in the hall of Wingate's house, a large, plush parlour which John usually visited only as a trader.

Wingate bore a grudge against the Puritans, as did many who had lost not only the war, but their estates and even their liberty. He himself had lost his father at the beginning of the Civil War and his mother had been forced to forfeit most of their estate to Parliament. He seemed to hold John personally responsible for his family's ruin, and had therefore not held back from arresting John although it would not be easy to charge him. Most of Wingate's contemporaries were slower and waited for the Act of Uniformity which forbade Non-Conformist worship and gave them more specific authority for a charge.

Wingate prepared to interrogate John, hoping to find something scandalous that could substantiate a charge. He began by asking the constable what the people had been doing when John was arrested. The constable could only reply that there were few people, that they had no arms or weapons with them and that as far as he could see they were doing very little. In short, there was no sign of a treasonable conspiracy.

For the sake of his pride, Wingate could not release John now. 'Why do you not content yourself with your calling as a tinker?' he asked him. 'It is against the law for such as you to preach.'

John replied that he counselled people to forsake their sins, draw near to Christ and avoid eternal damnation. He continued drily, 'I can manage both these without confusion, follow my calling and preach the Word also.'

Wingate's face darkened at what he suspected was insolence on the part of John. 'I will break the neck of your meetings.'

'Maybe so,' said John but he would not be threatened. Wingate ordered that John was to be bound over to keep the peace with sureties (similar to bail) until the next Hearing but Wingate insisted that he must not preach while he was free. This was to be a condition of his sureties. 'I shall break them then,' John said firmly, aware of the consequences of his words. 'I shall not leave preaching the Word of God.' He went on, angry at the injustice being perpetrated on him, 'I can't think that this is a work that harmful, but it's worthy of commendation rather than blame.'

'You will go to gaol then, until the Quarter Sessions.'

Each quarter the circuit Judges came to Bedford to judge the cases brought up in the previous three months; John was to wait in gaol until his case could be heard by these Judges. While the correct procedure was being followed to commit John to custody, he found himself the object of some self-righteous mockery. All those who had suffered silently the rules and austerity of the Puritan Republic now danced on Cromwell's grave and were gleeful at the downfall of the hated non-conformists. Dr Lindale, also staying at Wingate's house and probably part of the conspiracy against John, was one such man and, while John waited, he took his opportunity to taunt his captive. John at first tried to be rid of him by saying that he had come to talk to the Justice and not to him. Lindale took this to mean that John thought he was beaten and could say nothing in his defence. He laughed sarcastically, 'Have you taken oaths? Can you show me an authority for preaching? No, you don't have one, oh what a pity you'll have to go to gaol for it.'

John's patience broke and he snapped back, 'If I have a mind to I can answer any sober question you care to put to me.'

'How is it lawful for you to preach?' Lindale responded immediately. He was strong in his confidence of John's downfall. John quoted the Apostle Peter who said, 'As every man receiveth the Gift, even so let him minister the same.'

'And to whom is that spoken?' barked Lindale like an angry teacher seeking the right answer out of an unco-operative child.

'To whom?' said John. 'Why to every man that has received a gift from God.' John drew examples and began to preach, but Lindale smiled slyly and used an example from the New Testament that he knew would irritate John.

'In fact I remember that I have heard of one Alexander Coppersmith,' he underlined the name, hoping that the reference to trade would provoke John. 'This man did much to oppose and disturb the apostles.'

John was provoked despite himself, and retorted, 'I've read of many priests and Pharisees that had their hands in the blood of Jesus!'

'Yes! And you're one of them!' replied Lindale – they were

both losing their tempers now – 'for you with pretence, make long prayers and rob widows.' Here again was an accusation such as the one Edward Burrough, the Quaker, had levelled, that John preached for money and not from faith.

'If you earned money from preaching and praying,' argued John, 'you would not be so rich now!' He opened his mouth to say more and use his rhetoric to defeat his opponent, when a verse came into his mind: 'Answer not a fool according to his folly.' John paused and relapsed into a sullen silence, replying only a little so as not prejudice his case.

By this time the preparations to commit John to gaol had been made, and they got ready to go, but as they were leaving the house two friends met them and persuaded them to wait while they appealed to the Justice for one more night in which to come to a compromise. Their mission was successful, and John was told he could return to Wingate's house for a further night. Having once braced himself for gaol, John was reluctant to face instead another night of apprehensive waiting. He prayed as he returned that he would be given the strength not to do anything that would oppose the truth, for he feared to dishonour God and wound his conscience.

John was shown to a room in the house but as he was about to enter a man with a candle came out of the opposite room. It was Wingate's brother-in-law, a Dr Foster, and folk-lore has it that this was the Dr Foster who 'went to Gloucester in a shower of rain and stepped in a puddle right up to his middle and never went there again'. The story was that the streets of Gloucester were so rutted and wet, possibly flooded by the Severn, that the good doctor's carriage stuck fast and its occupant was half drowned! The rhyme was made up with some glee, for Foster was not a popular soul and his opposition to John was persistent and nasty in the years to come.

Foster greeted John as if he were a long lost brother, 'Who's there? John Bunyan?'

John was somewhat taken aback as he hardly knew Foster and what he had heard of him did not endear him to the man.

He wondered whether Foster had undergone a conversion; unfortunately this was not so.

John settled down to a drink and a chat with Foster. The polite small talk over, the drinks poured and the fire stoked, Foster got down to the real point. 'So,' he said. 'I understand that if you will promise not to call the people together again you shall have your freedom and instantly go home, for my brother is very loath to send you to prison.'

John smiled. He began to see the plan. 'I don't call the people together, they call me, all I do is exhort them to look after the salvation of their souls that they may be saved.' John started to explain the nature of salvation, and tried to sidetrack his protagonist by getting him to consider the state of his own eternal soul, but Foster was wise to that. 'We must not enter into explication and dispute now, but if you will say you won't call the people together, you may go free, if not, you must go to prison.'

'I shall not force or compel anyone to hear me, but if I come into any place where there are people met together, and they ask me, I should, according to the best of my skill and wisdom, exhort and counsel them to seek the Lord Jesus Christ, for the salvation of their souls.'

'You, John, should follow your calling!' Foster's façade was wearing thin. He told John that if he would only follow his calling as a tinker he would be acquitted. John would not shift, despite the temptation of freedom, and the thought of his young, heavily pregnant wife waiting, frightened and vulnerable, at home. He could not, while there were people who needed salvation, stop preaching. Foster's temper was growing short; it was important to his brother-in-law that this man Bunyan was turned from preaching. Such was the notoriety of John, even then, that if he stopped preaching the movement would be broken. 'Such meetings are against the law!' said Foster. 'Leave off, John, and call the people no more together.'

'I dare not make such a promise; for my conscience will not suffer me to do it. It is my duty to do as much good as I can, not only in my trade, but also to communicate to all people, wherever I meet them, the best knowledge I have of the Word.'

'You are nearer to the Papists than any!' Foster feared a nation of Catholics under Charles II, and he saw the failure of the Puritans to conform, to back the Anglican cause and their demands for tolerance as inadvertently paving the way for the Catholics. If John were allowed freedom to preach then so were they.

Coldly John asked, 'Why?'

'I will convince you of that immediately.' He paused, gathering his argument. 'You understand the scriptures literally?'

'Those to be understood literally, we understand literally, but for those that were to be understood otherwise we endeavoured so to understand them.'

'Which of the scriptures do you understand literally then?'

'He that believeth shall be saved, this is to be understood literally, according to the plain and simple words of the text.'

'You are ignorant, you don't understand the scriptures, how can you understand them when you don't know the original Greek?'

'Well, if that's your opinion, then none can understand the scriptures but those who had the original Greek, but then a very few of the poorest sort should be saved. This is too harsh, for scripture says, that God hides these things from the wise and prudent, that is from the learned of the world, and reveals them to babes and sucklings.

'None hear you but a company of foolish people!' Foster's frustration was no longer disguised.

So John went on, 'Wise and foolish hear me, and again those that are most commonly counted foolish by the world are the wisest before God. God has rejected the wise and mighty and noble and chosen the foolish and base.'

'You make people neglect their calling. God has commanded people to work six days and rest on the seventh. Rich and poor, all must look out for the welfare of their souls as well as for their bodies.' Being poor did not exclude people from the right to hear God's word.

Foster was losing the argument. He repeated to John that only foolish and ignorant people came to hear him. But John had a respect for such people that Foster did not share. He replied that they were as much in need of preaching as any man. Foster ignored this and returned to the original reason for beginning the conversation. He could see by then that John was determined to be the master of his own folly. He asked him once more if he would stop calling the people together. John said 'no' and Foster withdrew.

Later on that evening John was waited on by servants in the house who again assured him of the lenience of the magistrate. Despite their friendliness, John was now aware of the purpose of his remaining at the house, and did not shift his position. Foster returned with Wingate later on that evening and again they tried to persuade him to recant. Wingate clearly hoped to win a political victory by turning John aside. Foster, angered by John's stubbornness and his failure, revealed his true feelings for John and told Wingate that he should go to prison. So they gave up. As John went to the door he bit his tongue on pious words that would irritate his judge. 'I held my peace and blessed the Lord and went away to prison, with God's comfort in my poor soul.' It was the last door he was to open and shut freely for twelve years.

9

THE INDICTMENT

The moment the prison gates shut behind John he began immediately to apply for bail to get out, at least until the next Hearing. He had not seen Elizabeth or the children since the day he left to go to just one more preaching engagement. Now, by force, he was separated from them, trapped in a squalid gaol, damp and cold and under the eyes of all kinds of people; people he used to avoid in the street. His companions looked an unreceptive audience and John felt disinclined to introduce himself. He sat against the wall on a pile of straw, and picked and scratched at the floor. At last, helpless against the locks and bars of the prison, he put his head in his hands and began to pray. He prayed for strength and courage. He longed to get out again, but he knew he must accept God's will; all the same, he could hardly fight the tears, nor restrain the pleading with God to let him go free. At last he prayed for the success of his application for bail, but despite his efforts even that was refused, and for the most obscure of reasons.

His application went before a young man, Justice Compton, who was new to his job as a Magistrate. He had heard of John, but could not see why he had been sent to prison in the first place. There was no law, as yet, forbidding private meetings. He assumed therefore that there must be something more to the case than he was being allowed to know; some political misdemeanour perhaps. Whatever it was, Compton was convinced that it was serious and he would not let John go free. Thus John spent the seven weeks leading up to the Hearing in gaol.

This decision was made all the harsher by the circumstances in which John had left his family at a time when his support and presence were most needed. On the night of his arrest Elizabeth had waited apprehensively at home, trying not to let the children see her anxiety; at last there was that knock at the door. They came and told her as gently as they could that John had been arrested, going on quickly to say that there was hope for bail and that he was safe and well, but Elizabeth was too anxious. She could not control her terror any more. What was she to do with four children and a fifth on the way with no money and a husband in gaol or worse? How would she live without him? The cold doubt that had hovered in the back of her mind when John had left her that morning turned to a horror of his loss. It gripped her mind and her body, for now the child in her womb began to move and start its way, a month early, towards the light. The labour was brought on by the shock and the fears of a mother little more than a girl.

The children found themselves kept away from their adopted mother by friends and relatives, while their stepmother fought for her life and the life of her child, the first-born of her union with John. The children themselves waited in fear. Once again, they faced the possibility of losing not only their mother but also their father.

Elizabeth was in labour for eight terrible days. She suffered wild and irregular contractions with no hope of relief from pain, no grounds on which she could reassure the children. At last, exhausted and torn by worry at her helplessness, she gave birth to her child – but it was dead.

With the steadfastness of those who count their suffering as little in the Lord's work, Elizabeth recovered quickly but no one knows how close she came to death. An eight-day labour in the seventeenth century must have brought her to the brink of her endurance and once the child was born, the dangers of childbed fever, infection and haemorrhage were spectres haunting their home until she was well past the delivery. As for her grief, which was great, there was no husband to comfort her, or to look after the children and no help in her recovery. He was only a little way away but he

could have been on the moon for all the help he could give
her. Of course she visited him and the first time was a tearful
reunion, John, ridden with guilt, feeling responsible for what
had happened, and Elizabeth grieving for the loss of her
child, fearing the loss of her husband. They both longed for
one private moment in which to share their grief. It was not
the last time that John was to feel that being apart from his
family was as the flesh being torn from his body.

After seven weeks of waiting with the first-born of his new
marriage dead, and his wife still frail, John was brought to
trial at Bedford County Court. Sir John Kelynge was
chairman of the sessions, and there were four others on the
bench. Justice Kelynge could hardly have been a worse
Judge for John, for he had just spent eighteen years in gaol
for refusing to compromise on his Royalist sympathies. He
had waited a long time for an opportunity to return the
compliment to the Non-Conformists. Later he was to be
rebuked by his peers for being over-zealous in his
persecution of the Puritans.

By this time John's case had attracted some attention. He
was being made a scapegoat and the authorities determined
to make him an example to Bedford (a town dangerously
sympathetic to Parliament). He knew the seriousness of his
situation and was aware that he had to remain firm. He had
already committed himself and his future to God and came
to the Hearing prepared as he could be. He had had seven
weeks of doubt and grief to shake his resolve, but he was
convinced of the justice of his cause and aware of the
responsibility God placed upon him.

The Clerk of the Court rose and addressed John with the
charge 'That John Bunyan, of the town of Bedford,
labourer... devilishly and perniciously abstained from
coming to church to hear Divine service, and is a common
upholder of several unlawful meetings and conventicles to
the great disturbance and distraction of the good subjects of
this country...' the Clerk continued to read at length until at
last he said, 'What say you to this?'

John was careful with every word and replied, 'As to the

first part of it, I am a common frequenter of the Church of God. And I am also, by grace, a member with the people over whom Christ is the Head.' At this point Kelynge butted in, impatiently, 'Do you come to church, you know what I mean, to the parish church, to hear divine service?'

'No, I don't.'

'Why?'

'Because, I do not find it commanded in the Word of God.'

'We are commanded to pray.'

'But not by the Common Prayer Book.'

'How then?'

'With the Spirit,' John replied. 'As the apostle says, "I will pray with the Spirit, with understanding".'

The nub of John's argument with the authorities is to be found in that first exchange between John and Justice Kelynge. The Common Prayer Book was written by the Anglicans; it was to them the definitive theology. They believed that no individual could be trusted to formulate the correct doctrine by himself. If a man prayed with the Common Prayer Book he could not commit heresy. If he were allowed to make up his own prayers, soon Christianity would collapse in a cloud of different interpretations. So, Kelynge and his like insisted through the Law that all who went to prayer and worship did so in the Anglican Church with the help of the Prayer Book. But John replied that words were not a prayer, any heathen might speak his prayers, but he may not really feel or mean them, not really pray them. 'Show me,' he said, 'the place in the Epistles where the Common Prayer Book is written, or one text of scripture that commands me to read it, and I will use it.' He paused and went on, trying not irritate his Judge too much. 'They that have a mind to use it; they have their liberty. For my part I can pray to God without it.'

'Who is your God, Beelzebub?' accused one Justice.

John remained calm in all his replies to the interrogation. Kelynge tried one last assault with the verse of scripture that John himself referred to so often. '"As every man has received a gift even so let him minister the same, one to another ... if any man speak let him speak, as the oracles of God." Let me explain.' Kelynge was patronising in his attempt to be kind; he too saw the political capital to be gained in getting John to recant. 'As every man has received a trade, so let him follow it. If any man has received the gift of tinkering, as you have, let him follow his tinkering. And so other men their trades and the Divine his calling.'

John was in the process of explaining to Justice Kelynge that this interpretation of the verse did not fit with the verse that followed (and thereby showing a greater knowledge of the Bible than his opponent) when Kelynge, despairing of John's attitude, interrupted. 'We can wait for you no longer. Do you confess the indictment or don't you?'

John felt his nerves tighten. His resolve wavered, his mouth was dry and he shivered as he stepped towards the abyss. 'Now,' he says later 'and not until now, I saw I was indicted.' For the first time the impact of the situation had come home to him, the reality of what might happen to him. John could not argue or debate his way out of it now. In that silence at the end of the rapped-out question, John saw, with a dull pain in his heart, that he was, indeed, in trouble. He paused. This was definitely the time when he must throw himself on the mercy of God and pray for His strength and guidance.

'This I confess,' he said at last. 'We have had many meetings together, both to pray to God and to encourage one another, and that we had the sweet comforting presence of the Lord among us for our encouragement, blessed be His name.'

Kelynge replied, 'Then hear your judgment. You must be taken back to prison and stay there for three months, and at the end of three months if you do not submit, to go to church to hear divine service and leave your preaching, you must be banished from the realm and if after such a day you shall be found in this realm, or be found to have come over again without a special licence for it from the King, you must stretch by the neck for it'.

John was led back to gaol. The prospect of the gallows

faced him and the knowledge of at least three months in prison terrified him. Elizabeth caught his eye as he left the court. She was trying not to cry, but to smile. She looked so young, so ill, he could not but wonder whether his sacrifice should not have been borne alone? He wondered whether he should have remarried. Should a married man, a father, put himself in such a position when a family depended on him? Was it irresponsible? Should he have allowed himself to be bound over? He could not believe that he should. God had brought him to this point and surely His grace would prevail, give them all enough strength to go on. At that moment, however, he was not so sure.

10

THE APPEAL

Somewhere in the back streets of London, dark and poor, two men stalked. A man in middle age was coming towards them. The time was late and the night was cold. The man shuffled along hurriedly, fearful. The two men stepped forward to greet him. He stopped, keeping his head low, his eyes on the ground. The men examined him for a moment before speaking. Then one said, 'Who are you for?' The man shuffled, keeping his head low. He tried to assess the situation by examining their clothes. 'Who are you for?' repeated the stranger, his voice hardly hiding its sarcasm. The man mumbled hopefully, 'The King?'

'We,' said his antagonist slowly, but bitterly, 'are for King Jesus!' His voice rose, filled with hatred. He reached out to the terrified man who had dropped his bags and was backing away, trying to keep his head down, but the two of them held him hard. He struggled and screamed, a harsh grating cry that ended as abruptly as it had begun. They had cut off his head.

The cell door closed behind Paul Cobb, a messenger of the Court. John greeted him warmly. Amongst the many representatives of the Establishment Paul Cobb was a welcome sight. He was a sympathetic light in the dark wall of authority. John trusted that he had the best intentions towards him. Cobb sat down on the stool provided. He had not come that day with good news.

Cobb sighed and said, 'You see the late insurrection in London, how they pretended a holy cause, and yet indeed they intended no less than the ruin of the Kingdom and the Commonwealth.'

'I abhor that practice of theirs,' said John, only too aware of the effect that the behaviour of the Fifth Monarchists would have upon his case. The Fifth Monarchists felt that the turmoil of the age was leading to Christ's Second Coming. They believed that they alone had recognised this and were called, by God, to prepare the way for Christ's return. They were, ostensibly, a Puritan cult, and so in the eyes of the Royalists they were associated with people like John, who in reality was as far distant from their beliefs as he was from the Roman Catholics. But his grey Puritan clothes seemed to the courts to be reminiscent of the violent cult that threatened England's stability. The Fifth Monarchists were fanatics: they did not stop at sectarian murder, but tried to overthrow the King himself. All that was of little comfort to John, who carried on his defence. 'It doesn't follow because they did so therefore all others will do so. I look upon it as my duty to behave myself in the King's government, both as becomes a man and as a Christian, and if an occasion were offered me, I should willingly manifest my loyalty to my prince, both in what I do and say.' These words rang somewhat false in the ears of the Royalists for hadn't John Bunyan spent two years in the New Model Army, fighting against the King?

Cobb was genuinely concerned for John. He had already warned him that it would be worse for him in the next Hearing; he might well be banished or worse, but John believed that he had right on his side and he was becoming a skilled debater. Even after three months in gaol he could still argue his way round his opponents. 'If I may do good to one person only, by my preaching,' he argued, 'then why can't I do the same for two? And if two then why not four and so to eight?'

'Yes, and to a hundred as well I'll warrant you!' Cobb chuckled.

'Yes, why not? I don't think I should be forbidden to do as much good as I can.' Cobb had already conceded to John

that he could speak to his neighbour, so John had asked why
he could not hold private meetings? What was the
difference? Cobb returned to the insurrection of the Fifth
Monarchists to justify the King's ruling against such
meetings.

'Those people make their religion their pretence for they
really wish for disorder in the country, and so the law must
forbid private meetings, and tolerate only those held in
public. You may meet in public if you want.' But John saw
the trap in that; he could not hold a public meeting because
he had no licence to preach. A meeting might be safe but if he
opened his mouth just once his opponents could arrest him
again for preaching without a licence, so it had to be private
meetings, but now they too were forbidden.

'I speak the truth, Paul, and I'll go on speaking it, how can
that be wrong? I must defend my right to do so to the last
drop of my blood. Prove anything which I hold to be in error
and I will recant it.' He challenged Cobb like he challenged
Justice Kelynge, but Cobb, like so many others, felt it was
pointless of John to stand so firm now. He should just
compromise and wait, bide his time for an easier regime. At
the moment, the way he was going, he might well be hanged
for his right to speak.

Cobb sighed, 'You're a good man, John, but I think you
need not stand so strictly on this one point. Can't you submit
and not have meetings and then do as much good as you can
in a neighbourly way without such meetings?'

'But I am called to preach, commissioned by my Church. I
have a measure of light which God has given me, I dare not
but exercise that gift for the good of the people.'

Puritans were not known for expounding on their own
gifts and Cobb was annoyed by this seeming immodesty.
'Don't think you're so well enlightened, and that you have
received a gift so far above others.'

John returned to his verse that every man who has
received a gift must act accordingly.

'But,' said Cobb, 'what if you should forbear a while and
sit still, till you see how things will go?'

'Wycliffe says that he who leaves off preaching and hearing the Word of God, for fear of the excommunication of men, is already excommunicated of God and shall, in the Day of Judgment, be counted a traitor to Christ.'

'But how shall we know that you have the doctrine in the Bible?'

'Let any man hear and search and prove the doctrine by the Bible.'

'But will you be willing that two unbiased persons shall determine the case and will you stand by their judgment?'

'Are they infallible?'

'No,' said Cobb.

'Then it is possible that my judgment may be as good as theirs.'

'What about the Church?' Cobb was exasperated. 'Would you accept the judgment of the Church?' He was desperately looking for a way round the impasse that John faced as he dearly wanted to see John go free.

'Yes,' replied John, 'by the authority of scripture, no man is infallible.'

The argument continued for hours. Cobb had spent weeks trying to persuade John to compromise. They went over the issues again and again, trying to find a way out. Cobb felt strongly that John was wasting himself, possibly bringing about his own death and therefore denying the world his wisdom. What right had he to do that? But John would not compromise. He felt that if he let go of just one point then it would all collapse around him and he would have no strength for the other battles. He would, he knew, be riddled by guilt and thus lose his potency as a preacher and leader.

At last, ruefully beaten, Cobb got up to leave. He knew the situation was serious for John. There was no sympathy for the Puritans amongst the ruling powers, and John would not be co-operative. 'What benefit will it be,' speculated Cobb sadly, 'to you and your friends, what good can you do them if you should be sent only beyond the seas into Spain, or Constantinople or some other remote part of the world? Please, John, be ruled.'

The gaoler, who had come in to show Cobb out, caught the end of the conversation and said sternly, 'Indeed sir, I hope he will be ruled.'

But John would not co-operate, and he remained in gaol to face the consequences of his steadfastness: banishment or hanging.

His conditions in gaol were simple; a bed of straw and a stool and table. The cell was cold and damp, and only the warmest weather could make a difference to John's surroundings, but in a way it was quite civilised, unlike the notorious conditions of Newgate gaol where so many Puritans were imprisoned and found the filth and brutality overwhelming. Whatever the physical state of his one-window cell, his state of mind was severe. This was the man who had spent years agonising over the fate of his soul, who had become convinced that he was destined for hell, who had feared death as nothing else. Now, in gaol, he faced the possibility of death in reality rather than in theory. The vision of the gallows haunted his nights. Elizabeth was still frail. Who would provide for her if he were to be hanged? Should he choose to be hanged or banished? Would he be given the choice?

John had three months to mull over every dreadful possibility, three months in which the authorities intended that he should debate with himself over and over again the morality of what he was doing. They knew the potency of inner doubts. Should he let his family starve and suffer because he was arrogant enough to demand the right to preach? Should he trust God for his family and go to the gallows a martyr, wasted and silenced? The Establishment knew full well what agony of mind John suffered and it was their hope that it would break him; but he hung on, convinced that God had saved him for this and he must honour the martyrs and saints who had gone before him. He must honour the Church he was trying to build, honour the sacrifices and fears of the ordinary people who wanted a Puritan Church and needed leadership. He must not fear or waver, but how he wished that something, anything, would happen.

It was Cobb who brought a glimmer of light and a sense of activity into the dull cell, for on one of his visits he brought interesting news. King Charles II was to be crowned and it was the tradition on a coronation that there was an amnesty for certain political prisoners. Perhaps, suggested Cobb, John could apply for amnesty. From the day of the coronation prisoners had twelve months in which to apply for a pardon. On the day itself, many thousands of prisoners were released instantly, but John was not one of them. He had wasted no time in putting forward his application but, for the moment, there was no response to it. However, once his request was in, the courts could not touch him to carry out their sentence of banishment or hanging, so John remained in prison in continuing uncertainty until the Summer Hearing of 1661.

By this time John's wife was well again, a regular visitor to his depressing cell, and it was through her that John appealed to the Judges of the next Hearing. Elizabeth had to gather up all her strength and courage to carry out the commissions that John placed on her. Her first task was to travel to London to appeal for amnesty before Lord Barkwood at the House of Lords. It may well have been her first trip to London and certainly to the hallowed chambers of the House of Lords. Her request was debated but the chamber side-stepped the issue and told Elizabeth that only the Local Hearing at Bedford had the power to release John.

This set Elizabeth on the path of a series of appeals to the Judges on John's circuit. Sometimes in the months to come it was only her love for John that sustained her, and enabled her to step forward bravely and plead for her husband. Women, especially so young and humble, rarely spoke before such men of distinction and she was more than apprehensive. The first Judge she approached was Matthew Hale, whose reaction was not typical of others she received. He welcomed her and took her petition seriously, promising her gently that he would do what he could, but that it might not be very much. Encouraged by this, Elizabeth attempted to contact the second Judge, Judge Twisdon. He would not give her an appointment, but assuming that, like Hale, he

would not object to a direct approach, she tried another
route. Uninhibited, and fired by youthful desperation,
Elizabeth waited for Twisdon on his route into chambers.
When she saw his carriage approach, she realised she could
not safely stop it. She had only one opportunity and she took
it. She flung her petition into the carriage, where it landed on
Judge Twisdon's lap.

Twisdon stopped the carriage and opened the door. He
ordered the apprehensive young woman in. He was furious
and testily informed her that John was convicted and could
not be released until he stopped preaching. Downhearted
and shaken by the Judge's anger, Elizabeth watched the
carriage depart. It seemed possible that by her flamboyant
and youthful action she had made things worse for John.
Perhaps now the angry Judge would demand the carrying
out of the sentence of hanging. She went home, agonising
over the possibilities, afraid to tell John of what she had
done. She felt that all hope was lost, and that afternoon she
could not hold back the tears as she told him of her
humiliation. It was only John's gentle reassurance and slight
amusement that restored her strength and morale. They
decided she should go again to Judge Hale, as he had given
her a sympathetic hearing the first time. So she applied once
more to him and was given a hearing during sessions. She
appealed for mercy, but Hale's colleague on the bench,
Judge Chester, snapped across her saying, 'John Bunyan is a
hot-spirited fellow and convicted in the court.' Hale,
although sympathetic, was overwhelmed by the opinions of
his fellows and the weight of the law; but Elizabeth did not
give up.

She managed to gain entrance to the Swan Chamber,
where the Judges rested and heard petitions between
sessions. She was terrified of facing so many distinguished
and clever men by herself. She had had little education and
she felt she did not have John's gift of advocacy. Women
were not expected to take the lead in her society. How was
she going to persuade such powerful men? She started on
Judge Hale as he seemed the easiest opponent. 'My Lord,

may I make bold once again to know what will happen to my husband?' Hale was by now irritated by her persistence and he seemed embarrassed at being appealed to in front of his peers.

'Woman,' he said curtly, 'I told you before, I can do you no good, because they have taken what your husband said at the sessions for a conviction. Unless there is something that will undo that, I cannot help you.' He emphasised the last words firmly, hoping that she would take the hint and leave at last, but she stayed where she was.

'My Lord, he is kept in prison unlawfully. They clapped him in gaol before there were any proclamations against the meetings, the indictment is false. Besides, they never asked him whether he was guilty or not and he didn't confess the charge.'

Another Judge whom Elizabeth had not seen before, was listening near by. He moved nearer and said to Hale, 'My Lord, he was lawfully convicted.'

'That's false,' exclaimed Elizabeth indignantly, 'for when they said to him, "Do you confess the indictment?" he could only say that he had been to several meetings, both where there was preaching the Word and prayer and that they had God's presence with them.' She was grasping at straws, for she was suggesting that as all such meetings were called by a general consensus and were held in equality, with no particular person singled out, no one man could be held responsible for them.

Twisdon now decided to contribute. His hostility towards Elizabeth was no less than before and he did not try to hide it. He asked whether she thought they, as Judges, could do as they please, as if they were not bound by the law. 'Your husband is a breaker of the peace,' he went on, 'and so convicted by the law.'

Hale, however, was not convinced. Elizabeth was obviously genuinely disturbed, and perhaps an injustice had been done. He called for the Statute Book, to check the legality of John's conviction, and while they waited she reiterated her claim. 'He was not lawfully convicted.'

'My Lord, he was lawfully convicted,' rebutted Judge Chester, joining in the debate.

'It's not true,' said Elizabeth again as she and Chester glared at each other.

Chester took refuge in the written word. 'But it is recorded, woman, it's recorded!'

Elizabeth, aware that since the verdict was recorded she would get no further trying to persuade them that it was false, tried another argument. 'My Lord, I was in London not long ago, to see if I could get my husband's freedom.' She described her petition to Lord Barkwood and their claim that only the Local Hearing could release John. She hoped an influential name might cause the Judges to think twice, but they were now trying to ignore her and did not reply. She did not know if they had even heard what she had said. She stood by, uncertainly, wondering whether she should say more or whether she had been dismissed. At last Chester repeated, 'It is recorded.'

'It is false!' said Elizabeth near to tears.

Chester, exasperated by her, appealed to Hale who was still thoughtful. 'He is a pestilent fellow, there is no one else like him for trouble!'

Twisdon suddenly turned on her venomously. He had a strange habit of prefacing much of what he said with the word 'what' and he did it now, startling Elizabeth. 'What! Will your husband stop preaching?'

'My Lord,' she stammered back, 'he dare not leave preaching as long as he can speak.'

'See here,' Twisdon tried to intimidate her, but Elizabeth's young and hopeful face remained firm. 'What! Should we talk any more about this? Must he do what he likes? He is a breaker of the peace.' She tried to reassure him that all they wanted to do was to live in peace. 'I have four small children that cannot help themselves, one of them is blind and we have nothing to live on but the charity of good people.'

Hale's suspicions were aroused; four children by one so young? Was she deceiving him with her sad story?

'How have you four children?' he asked sternly.

Elizabeth realised the incongruity of what she had just said, and she hurried to retrieve her credibility. 'I am but mother-in-law to them, not having been married to John for two years. Indeed,' she went on, the pain of her own personal hurt welling inside her and reflected on her face, 'I was with my own child when my husband was first apprehended, but being young and unused to such things, I was dismayed by the news and went into labour, and so continued for eight days and then was delivered,' she paused, 'but my child was dead.'

Hale turned, aware that there was authenticity in this woman's hurt. 'Poor woman,' he murmured.

There was a pause, but Twisdon's boorish mind saved the Judges from their guilt. 'You make poverty your cloak, woman,' he accused her and went on to say that she would not be suffering such misfortune if her husband had followed his calling.

'What is his calling?' asked Hale.

'A tinker, my Lord,' replied someone helpfully. Everyone, it seemed, had heard of John Bunyan.

'Yes!' replied Elizabeth defiantly, 'and because he is a tinker, a poor man, he gets no justice.' She raised her voice, nervous but angry. It was a revolutionary accusation and could have finished her case there and then.

There was a moment's silence and then Hale laughed. He was not offended and he took her aside a little way from the academic debate of the Judges. 'I tell you, woman, seeing that they have taken what your husband said as a conviction, you must either apply yourself to the King or sue out a pardon, or get a writ of error.'

Hale did not succeed in keeping his counsel from the others and Chester was indignant. 'My Lord, he will preach and do what he likes!'

'He preaches nothing but the Word of God!' Elizabeth retorted.

'He, preach the Word of God?' mocked Twisdon, and Elizabeth was at the centre of their arena again. She was frightened that Twisdon would hit her, he seemed so enraged. 'He runs up and down and does harm.'

Elizabeth stood her ground, 'When we come to Judgment Day my husband will be vindicated.'

'Don't take any notice of her,' Twisdon insisted, 'send her away.'

Hale turned to her with a helpless look. 'I'm sorry I can't do anything for you. You must do one of those things I said; either apply to the King, sue out a pardon or get a writ of error. A writ of error will be cheapest,' he added, knowing her circumstances.

Elizabeth tried one more angle; could not John himself be brought to them there, to plead his own case and defend his own appeal? But they wanted no more to do with it. There was nothing else to be said. Elizabeth had failed John and his children. She felt totally inadequate; if only it could be the other way round; she in gaol and he free, then they might have had some chance, but she could not measure up to John's skill and she had not the faith to work miracles. She stood in the doorway of the chamber unable to stem the tears any longer. She cried for her lost child and for her imprisoned husband; but most of all, she cried for justice.

11

THE DESERT YEARS

John and Elizabeth waited and persisted but the authorities presented the couple with a wall of silence. It seemed to John that both he and Elizabeth were in prison. John would work at leather laces in prison, while Elizabeth sewed by the light of a dying candle flame at home; although they were just a few miles apart, they were imprisoned by their separation. John felt as if he had pulled his house and home down upon his head and on the heads of his family. He beat against the prison walls, trying to gain release with growing desperation, but the twelve-month waiting period for his pardon passed, and the King offered him no reprieve. Once again the visions of the gallows and banishment haunted John and he longed for the situation to be resolved as soon as possible. He knew that the Quarterly Hearings were due in Bedford, so he put his application in to be heard but to no avail. Although the bureaucrats were not inclined to follow through a sentence of banishment or death on John, they did not want him free either, so they stood together and ignored him.

John was to spend a good part of twelve years in gaol, sometimes alone, sometimes sharing his cell with an abundance of Non-Conformists. At first John's experience of prison did not entail constant confinement. The demands on him were such that a lenient gaoler allowed him out occasionally, on the surety of his own word to return. This was before the Summer Hearing at which Elizabeth worked so hard; and John took the opportunity not only to visit his family, but to visit friends and members of the fellowship who needed him. Not only that, he also indulged in the crime which had put him in gaol in the first place – preaching. But this flexibility was short-lived; John's absence from prison was noticed and the gaoler was warned not to let it happen again. So the gates closed on John finally and were not (even slightly) opened for several years.

A friend, John Holden, a fellow brazier and perhaps a partner, took care to see that Elizabeth and the children did not go hungry. Elizabeth could not visit John every day as she had enough work to do cultivating their small field and looking after the family. Sometimes she would go to the prison alone and they would discuss the problems between herself and her stepchildren; sometimes she would bring the children with her. Their conversations took place in the squalid surroundings of John's cell, confined by the limited visiting time. Elizabeth brought food and clothes to John but as he took them he could not help wondering what sacrifices she was making to provide for him, when he should be providing for her. In the last few minutes of visiting before Elizabeth had to leave, they would sit talking about anything other than their imminent separation. Sometimes it was all she could do to hold back the tears, and John could hardly bear the thought of the lonely hours ahead. He dare not watch her as she gathered herself and her things together once more, to leave him alone in the prison. When she had gone, he would pace the prison cell, stamping as if he were cold, moving constantly, finding refuge from his pain in activity.

However, despite their shared and individual suffering, John was not as austere and miserable as might be expected of someone who found himself indefinitely imprisoned for an undefined crime. When the doors finally closed behind him and he could no longer hope for an early release, when there were no visitors and few who wished to listen to him or talk with him, he turned his back to his old skills as a tinker. Quietly in his cell he detached a leg from the stool he was provided with and carved holes in it in what he approximated was the correct order and distance apart and just as he had made a metal violin for his children, he now made a flute from the leg of a stool. He sat on his straw bed, playing quietly to himself the hymns and choruses they had sung at the meeting places. The sound floated down to his gaoler who sat by the fire dozing. At first he thought the sound came from outside or was a part of his dream, but as he gradually woke up, he realised that it was no dream flute and that it was coming from inside the prison. In fact, he could swear that it was coming from John Bunyan's cell. Grumbling, he picked up his candle and clattered his way noisily to the cells. The sound stopped at his approach. He went on, uncertain. Was his mind playing tricks? Was there a ghost? Was some mournful, unjustly accused prisoner of a bygone age luring him to his death? He peered through the slats on the heavy oak door of John's cell. John was sitting on a stool, a candle on the table, poring over one of the two books he possessed. The gaoler looked again, and he could detect a slight shaking in the prisoner's shoulders. Was John Bunyan weeping or laughing?

Prison was rarely relieved by the occasional prank, it was a harsh frightening world for John. At night he saw himself mounting the gallows. 'I thought I would be ashamed to die with a pale face and knocking knees.' It was his greatest terror that if called upon to suffer martyrdom, he would not be able to meet it with nobility. He tried to visualise himself meeting his death with dignity, he tried to rehearse what he would say, but as the nights passed and still no hangman came for him, he began to relax and adjust himself to a long – possibly life-long – prison sentence.

As part of the experience of being in prison, John found himself drawn to his old adversaries, the Quakers. A man called John Rush was arrested with one Thomas Greene and they were brought to Bedford gaol two months after John himself was imprisoned there. These two Quakers, much to John's annoyance, proceeded to write *A Few Plain Words to the Inhabitants of England*, a tract on behalf of the Quakers. They were a captive audience for John, to whom he could preach and who preached in their turn. They passed the time in debate, sometimes heated, John believing his opponents to be erring dangerously near to heresy and the others desperately trying to prove otherwise.

The Quakers were young, well bred and used to a comfortable life, unlike the rustic tinker who had served in the army, pounded the lanes around Bedford in all weathers and had worked late into the night with unyielding metal. The Quakers were unprepared for the physical strains prison life put on them. Rush fell ill with a strange kind of gaol fever that consumed him like a fire. Despite all their efforts to help him they were powerless against the disease, and the conditions in which they were kept hindered everything they did. John watched the life of the young Quaker slip away. He died on January 11th, 1662 in the depths of winter on a pile of damp straw. John and his fellows prayed at his side and then called for the gaoler; for all his emnity with the Quakers, John could not but grieve for the life of this faithful and earnest young man. They faced the beginning of 1662 with fear and depression.

Although life for John in gaol was dismal, it was, at least, consistent. In a very real way, the worst had happened to him, whereas for his fellows outside the situation was precarious and getting worse. The authorities, after a slow start, were clamping down on what they saw as a possible source of a future uprising. The Act of Uniformity insisted that all churches and their ministers conformed under the umbrella of the Anglican Church. The Bedford congregation were dispossessed of their remaining meeting houses, William Dell was ejected from his pulpit and retired to Samsell, where John had been arrested, in dismal anticipation of further repression; Oliver Cromwell's principal preacher would never see such tolerance again. Others, such as John Donne of Pertenhall, younger and more energetic than Dell, retreated to the woods and fields where services were held.

In 1664, as a result of the actions of people like John Donne, a new Conventicle Act was instituted. This forbade any religious meetings except those held by the Anglican Church. But this was not enough, so the Five Mile Act was instituted, which forbade illegal ministers the right to live within a five-mile radius of any corporate population. In some ironic way this might have boosted the Puritans, for many of the dissenters were probably saved from the Great Plague, when it came, because of their distance from infected areas. Nevertheless the hardship was severe, many teachers with Puritan leanings lost their jobs and many lost their homes and livelihoods, for they suffered fines of up to £40 – perhaps £5,000 in today's terms.

The Non-Conformist Church was suffering a storm of persecution and while John remained in gaol he was not only visited by many, but the monotony was broken by the arrival of other Puritans. They were often in good spirits despite their predicament. One of John's early biographers tells of when he first met John. He went to visit him in gaol when it was full of Puritans, for John Donne had been preaching, as was his habit, in Keysoe woods and unfortunately he and his congregation were arrested and placed in Bedford gaol – all sixty of them. 'And so,' says the biographer, 'the prison was very crowded, and yet in the midst of it all I heard Mr Bunyan both preach and pray with the might of the Spirit and faith... that made me stand and wonder.'

So John had a chance to exercise his ministry of preaching, and the crowded prison was more like a church than a gaol. The ordinary felons must have often wondered what kind of criminals shared their cell.

However, for John there was still no escaping the fact that he was not released with the apparent ease that the other Non-Conformists were. A few Puritans might join him on his way and they would sing and laugh together, in the hope of better days, but soon, one by one, they would turn and say goodbye, leaving John alone. He had been picked out as an example to others, so he remained imprisoned, uncertain. The visits of his fellow prisoners could not compensate for the fact that his children were growing up without him, that his body, despite his regime of exercise, was wasting and growing older and his morale was often so low that he wished for death to release him and Elizabeth from this intolerable way of life.

It was at this time that, in order not to submit to the depression which sometimes threatened to defeat him, John started writing again. His first tracts against the Quakers had been successful so he tried his hand at some Puritan theology. He wrote reams, expounding on the scriptures, morality, behaviour, the Holy Spirit and Non-Conformist interpretations of the Bible. His books sold well; he may not have been able to preach in the open but he certainly had not been silenced. His writing grew popular, and his own autobiography *Grace Abounding to the Chief of Sinners*, describing his path of martyrdom was successful too. John's voice was becoming more powerful than it ever was when he was free and the authorities did not fail to respond. They hit back in 1666. John's publisher and his premises were raided, and among the books confiscated was *Grace Abounding*. The suppression had begun. The Anglican Establishment, if not the King, was desperate to still John's voice, but they stopped short of execution.

12

COMETS, PLAGUES AND FIRE

High in the sky, visible to all, a light began to make its presence felt; a wonder of space, like the Star of Bethlehem, appeared in the depths of December in 1664. This revelation, to a still ignorant race only just beginning to understand their universe, could only mean disaster. That comet was followed in March, by a second, lesser comet. Neither of these was Halley's comet, although Halley himself watched and studied these two messengers of heaven; the comet to which he was to lend his name was not to arrive until 1682, while John was still alive. It was, however, Halley's comet, as it became known, that was most responsible for causing people to think that comets heralded doom. It is depicted in the Bayeux Tapestry, for one of its appearances took place in the year of the Norman Conquest. While Halley studied the science of these unusual phenomena, the people, unaware of the dawn of the scientific age, contemplated apprehensively the meaning of these visions. To whom did their message apply? What disaster would be carried in their wake?

They did not have long to wait, for almost as soon as the last sight of its tail disappeared, the Great Plague began. To many this was a visitation from God, a direct reprimand for putting a king like Charles II on the throne. They looked back to the good old days, telling each other that such a thing would never have happened in the days of Cromwell. By September 1665, seven thousand one hundred and sixty-five Londoners had died of the Plague, hardly a family was left untouched and no one living in London could fail to witness the isolated streets, the bodies or avoid hearing the tales of pain that drove men mad and sent them shrieking down the streets calling upon heaven to administer mercy. The Angel of Death passed over London and looked towards Bedford, which was filled with dread anticipating the first sign of the illness.

For those in prison trapped close to one another, in damp, dirty and miserable conditions, separated from their loved ones, it was a living hell, such as the one John had once feared. They were overtaken by a sense of doom and terror; each prisoner was watching and waiting, every late visit of a relative froze the heart of the one who waited. Every cough and pain was regarded with suspicion by those who watched their glands constantly for the first swelling signs of the Plague. John was torn apart by worry, sometimes in anguish over Elizabeth and his children, sometimes rocked with fear for himself. But he still maintained his reputation as a courageous man and, in the unofficial post of pastor to his Church, he had to try to soothe his frightened congregation, while his own temples pulsed with anxiety.

A bitterly cold winter halted the march of death northwards and Bedford was allowed a stay of execution while they waited uncertainly for the warmth of spring. In 1666 as the sun turned back towards the north, forty people were taken by the disease which broke out in the area of the prison. It was the hardest time for John and Elizabeth since the first months of their separation. They dared not see each other while the disease raged around the prison. They decided that Elizabeth should keep as far away as she could from the infected area, so she waited and worked in her cottage, almost frantic with worry. She had to live in ignorance of what was happening to John, only assuming that no news was good news. She resented the authorities that kept them apart. Would this imprisonment never end? Others were out, free, but not John. John had been her husband for only two years before he was taken from them, and now he faced mortal danger without her. Separated and frightened, they survived unscathed, although friends and acquaintances succumbed. They did suffer one particular loss that year, although not to the Plague, for the preacher whose sermon on the playing of games had so convinced John all those years ago, died.

The Plague's fury ravaged on, leaving those remaining to rebuild and survive. Hardly a year had elapsed however when the following famous entry was made by Samuel Pepys in his diary: 'The saddest sight of desolation that I ever saw, everywhere great fires, oil cellars, and brimstone, and other things burning. I became afraid to stay there long, and therefore down again, the fire being spread as far as I could see.' Pepys witnessed the Great Fire of London from the top of Barking Steeple before he fled from its path. The Fire had swept through the tinder-dry streets with remarkably little loss of life, but the damage was extensive. It destroyed medieval London, it ended an age.

London learned from its mistakes and began to construct a more robust city in place of the old one. The fire was an economic disaster and for John, emerging from these years relatively unscathed, it had been a harsh censor. Much of his work was lost in the fire.

Nevertheless some advantage was to be gained from these disasters for panic had gripped the town of Bedford. First the Plague and now the Fire. Would this grief never finish? Was the world preparing for its end? The Second Coming of Christ? Families wanted to be together, in case further disasters would befall the town and the world. The prison staff of Bedford were no exception and John was allowed limited freedom for a few weeks, while they retreated to their families.

At last John could walk again in the country lanes around Bedford and view the changes in the town. At last he could polish up his old tools, even earn a bit of money for his wife and mend those things in the house that needed mending. He could visit his friends instead of having them come to see him. They were overjoyed to see the reassuring figure of John, his red hair now tinged with grey, standing on their doorstep, ready and willing for some refreshment and a chat.

By now John had suffered the refiner's fire; his character,

once so agonised in pre-conversion, then so enthusiastic as a
preacher and so defiant as an internee had acquired the
mellow strength of a patient man. He could face what his
cause might bring and he ministered to his people simply by
being with them again. Most of all he could be with his
family, his children, his blind Mary, and his sons, growing
up without him. He and his boys walked together and talked,
they shared their lives with the immediacy that was lost when
he was in prison. It was an age since he had been free,
another life.

It was a chance, too, for John to take Elizabeth in his arms
again, the wife he had hardly had a chance to be husband to,
especially in her most desperate time, the wife for whom he
had wept when she had lost their child, the guilt of which he
would always carry, the wife for whom he had suffered in
terror as the news that the Plague had reached Bedford had
been brought to him. He had feared that he would never see
her again, but he did, and he had not long been taken back to
prison when Elizabeth came to tell him that soon a child
would be born to them. The cold frosts of the spring of 1666,
and the knowledge of a further separation was made both
harder and easier in the knowledge that their child, Sarah,
would give Elizabeth the fulfilment as a mother she had been
denied all those years ago.

The Plague and the Fire in a morbid way alleviated one of
the most pernicious aspects of John's prison life, monotony.
Despite the suffering he experienced as he feared for his
congregation and family, at least there had seemed to be
some movement in the nation. Now he faced a further period
of prison life without indication as to how long it would last,
or even whether it would end on the gallows as he had once
feared. He wrote little in the next six years as he waited. In
fact those years are missing years in his life, recorded in his
own pilgrimage as his wilderness years.

The atmosphere in the country was less conducive to
publishing his works. Francis Smith his printer had been
raided and John's books were confiscated. The restrictions
on publishing further undermined his existence in prison,

for what hope was there if he could not even write and communicate? What point was there to this silent martyrdom? Seven, eight, nine years of gaol, with any number to come, was a discouraging prospect for even the most devoted of men. His family were growing up, making more demands on his time and his earning capacity. The Church looked to him for pastoral help, but he was not free and there was no substitute for freedom, no greater reward and no yearning as strong.

While John began to wonder if he was to remain in gaol until his mind and body rotted, the Non-Conformist Church outside battled against the repression and fear that bound them. John already suffered the consequences of his stand, but the people outside saw his steadfastness not just as an encouragement but as a warning of the punishment in store for them. The nation, too, hankered after easier days. A nostalgia manifested itself, which Pepys recorded in his diary with a sense of disbelief. Pepys was a staunch supporter of the Restoration, and found the fun-loving Charles II far more to his taste than the austerity of Cromwell. 'It is strange,' he said, 'how everybody do nowadays reflect upon Oliver Cromwell and comment him, what brave things he did and made the neighbour princes fear him; while here a prince come in with all the love and prayers and good liking of his people, that lost all so soon, that it is a miracle what way a man could devise to lose so much in so little time.'

In 1670, the Non-Conformist Church although reluctant was still rebellious and found itself under attack; for if the people were steadfast in remaining non-conformists then Dr William Foster was as keen as ever to stop them. A further new Conventicle Act fuelled Foster's zeal. This act banned religious meetings not only in a public place but in private homes. Foster discovered that nine homes, termed hearths, were used in Bedford for such meetings, and he set about finding these homes. Those who could not pay faced gaol.

On May 20th, 1670, when John had been in gaol for ten years and just ten days after the new Conventicle Act had become law, the situation in Bedford erupted and the people joined together in protest. The law had assaulted the Englishmen's castles and they were tired of the years of constant harassment and fear.

A certain Thomas Battison, an elderly churchwarden of St Paul's, Bedford, was appointed by Foster to collect the fines owed, but the people of Bedford gave Thomas Battison a good deal of work to do. Unsuspecting, he called first to collect the fine from John Bardolfe's Malt House. Battison was to take the fines in kind if money could not be offered, but John Bardolfe had pre-empted him and had sold his malt the previous day. Battison was unsure as to the legality of his position, and did not feel that he could enter Bardolfe's house and exact a fine by force. He stood discussing this problem with his fellow helpers and a group of interested and animated people gathered around him in the High Street. The disturbance was sufficient to indicate to those in the prison that something untoward was happening in the town. John heard the noise and later listened to the details from Elizabeth with amused curiosity.

Battison decided to move on to the grocer's shop; one Edward Coventon owned that. He had been known among the Bedford congregation as something of a backslider and earlier in the same year had been reprimanded on this subject by John himself. However, with all eyes upon him, Coventon stood firm and refused to pay the fine of five shillings that was levied against him. Battison was, by this time, frustrated and embarrassed, and angrily he confiscated a brass kettle in lieu of the fine. He then called a little boy of about nine to him and paid the boy sixpence (a fair sum then) to carry the kettle to the Inn Yard. The boy had to earn his sixpence, for he ran a gauntlet of hissing and booing locals who lined the route to the Yard. They were by now so vociferous that when he reached the Inn gate the publican was there to meet him. He feared for his property and, inspired by the spirit of protest in the crowd, he refused to let the kettle pass. The boy felt he had done enough for his sixpence so he dropped the kettle and ran. One of the publican's men was instructed to take the kettle into the middle of the road, where the crowd surrounded it, waiting for Battison's next move. A stalemate had been reached and Battison withdrew to seek further help from Foster.

He did nothing until the following day, which was a Sunday, when he decided to catch the meetings in full swing and so justify the forceable exacting of the fines. The fines were also doubled and Battison, armed with that threat and a few men, entered the meetings but everyone flatly refused to be intimidated. Battison sent a message to Foster to that effect. Foster sent a curt message back instructing Battison to co-opt help for the task from the gentlemen of the town. Battison enlisted a few unwilling souls to come from their Sunday lunches and troop all the members of the meetings to the Swan Chamber. There, their names were taken and they were kept until four o'clock in the afternoon, by which time the captors could bear their prayer and piety no longer.

Battison, by now regretting his authority, went home and the next morning not only he, but Foster, some constables and soldiers, marched up the streets of the town attempting to enlist more help from the gentlemen of the town. Most of these, by now forewarned, sent messages of regret, for they had all mysteriously found urgent business out of town that day, and would that Monday be unavailable to help. The party was undeterred and, led by Battison, commenced their duty and first knocked on the door of Thomas Honeylove. They did not stay there long however, for one look at Honeylove's children told them that there was smallpox in the house, and they beat a hasty retreat, empty-handed. Their next attempts were more successful: they took three loads of wood from the local heel-maker, the best coat from the tanner, the household goods and all the materials of his trade from the local pipe-maker (whose fame in the area was widespread). A wealthy widow was fined twenty pounds and they took all her valuable goods including the sheets from her bed. This was a particularly harsh fine and the last straw; the people now decided to boycott the soldiers and Battison. They closed their doors on him and hid themselves and their goods and were simply out when Foster himself came to call. This ploy worked temporarily at least, and for the time being Foster had to retreat. A pamphlet that described these events was the first to set down the principles of non-violent resistance, a statement of policy which was later made famous by Gandhi.

In the long term the people did not win, but for the first time in ten years John felt that there at last was hope that the pendulum would swing. Could such a movement as Puritanism ever be permanently silenced when it once had freedom? Perhaps there was yet hope that in his lifetime he might see a movement of the people that would bring about freedom of religion.

It was however a brief interlude in the tedium of his life. He was becoming paralysed by boredom and disillusion without hope. He knew he was growing sour, he could write little and, it seemed, he laughed less. He would pace his cell and pour out his troubles to Elizabeth, who sat patiently nursing her child, trying to get him interested in the individual they had created together. Sometimes John caught an expression on her face and remembered how hard and lonely it was for her. Then he would smile and encourage her in her own struggle. He would hear of the children's latest mischief; they did not visit as often as they used to. He advised her on how to cope but he was a father by proxy and sometimes he was at a loss as to what to suggest, and then all the frustration returned, all the impatience and the hurt at the injustice broke once more. They would part with an unsatisfactory embrace, and once she was gone, John thudded his fist into the prison wall in anger, crying out to God to let him go free or die, anything to take him out of the twilight of his present existence.

However overtaken by despair, John was a disciplined man, capable of pulling himself out of his own 'Slough of Despond'. Gone were the days when he agonised over the nature of faith and the uncertainty of salvation. Now confident of that, at least, he could be the master of his own morale and he would hide his boredom in those lost years by involving himself in the problems of the small Bedford congregation.

It's clear from the Church records that John was a growing influence on the fellowship. They were hard, discouraging years and the congregation lived under the threat of prison fines and general harassment; such an atmosphere provoked its own strains. The people were committed to a cause that was anti-Establishment, they had to make sacrifices for that cause and however strong the opposition, stick together, espouse the same theology and show the same commitment. Individualism, although encouraged by the Non-Conformists, was also a threat. There were, even in this movement, restrictions and conformity and John was a mainstay of the developing theology in the Church and because of this he had gained the trust and respect of the congregation.

The strain was too much for some though, and they slipped from the straight and narrow; so the Church expended some effort in trying to encourage their wayward brethren to return to the fold. John was often called upon to speak to the culprits. He did this by letter from his prison cell and sometimes they came to visit him and share their doubts.

In 1668 the Church agreed that a certain Samuel Ffenne, John Ffenne and John himself should speak with a certain Robert Nelson and admonish him for his withdrawal from the Church and other failings. In the same meeting it was decided that John should speak to Edward Coventon and reprimand him. Edward Coventon did return to the fold to make his stand in the battle of the kettle, but John's ministerings were not so successful with others. Brother Merrill, for instance, failed to conform to the Church's way; 'as for brother Merrill,' the Church records state, 'though their words and carriage were so winning and he did not become impatient and break out into that impatience as he had sometimes done, yet after some talking he began in an obscure way to charge the Church with rebellion and also with taking some portions of scripture that are made for their purposes and refusing the other.'

That entry was recorded on October 14th, 1669 but on
January 21st, 1670, despite their constant pleadings and
admonitions, 'Humphrey Merrill was cut off from, and cast
out of this Church of Christ'. He had broken the covenant
with God and his fellowship for he recanted his Puritan faith
at the General Quarter Sessions and generally accused the
Non-Conformists of the crimes for which the Establishment
fined them. The pressure had been too much for Humphrey
Merrill and he collapsed and went to the other side, perhaps
less out of conviction than fear. John's signature was on the
document that ostracised this man from the fellowship, as it
was on the document that cut off Richard Deane from the
congregation.

This man had done a good deal to bring the fellowship
into disrepute. Amongst the charges brought against him
was that of fraud: 'Selling several persons deceitful goods.'
He also went from door to door in the villages and towns
begging for charity, claiming that amongst others the money
would be given to John in gaol. This he did without John's
knowledge and not to his benefit. Such behaviour was
extremely damaging to the congregation. They all suffered
the persecution attached to their Puritanical beliefs and if
one was shown to be a fraud, or immoral or of general bad
character, the consequences of that bad reputation would
denigrate the whole congregation and their cause.

The vice gripped harder and the Church was more severely
threatened with every new Act of Parliament. It seemed the
Anglicans were getting their own way with the King. Many
people had to leave their families and flee to live outside the
towns as a result of the 'Five Mile Act'. These people were
not so used to separation and suffering as John, so as well as
his more arduous duties John wrote letters from prison to his
frightened, scattered flock. He encouraged them to remain
steadfast and he did so from the position of one who could
really claim to understand.

'God is wise,' he said to one brother Harrington, who was
separated from his family. 'He does all things for the best, for
them that love Him.' John's years in gaol enabled him to say

with certainty that God knew best. He pointed out that in the future they would look back and understand what God was doing leading them along this rocky path. But sometimes, as he wrote these words, John wondered what he himself was doing encouraging people to stand fast and live separate from their family. To do so, some people put everything they had in jeopardy; was he irresponsible in telling them to go ahead? Was he asking too much of them? Would they fail under the strain? In his heart, he knew he did not always see God's wisdom in all this and sometimes he really did not know what it was all for.

13

FAMILY AND FREEDOM

A colossal storm raged above the town of Bedford. The inhabitants fled to the safety of their homes while the wind and rain lashed against their walls. The lightning cracked the sky with a noise like ripping cloth. The superstitious people had never seen anything like it before and they cowered before it. The fears and memories of the comets were still too recent for them to see anything other than a bad omen in the storm. A tree was ripped from its roots and thrown like a feather as high as the church steeple. John and his family stayed in their small cottage, listening and praying together. John was at last out of prison, and this was the one ordeal that he did not have to leave his family alone to face. Now he could be there, encouraging them, soothing the children, holding frightened hands, brushing tears away from terrified faces, and occasionally checking the cottage and its structure to make sure that it was not suffering serious damage. There were moments, though, as the wind lashed at the door and the thunder sent the children screaming to their mother, when John wondered whether he had been released simply to share the end of the world with his family.

John had left prison earlier that year. On March 15th, 1672, a Declaration of Indulgence was announced by King Charles II. The extra pressures of the past two years were suddenly alleviated and the Puritans could breathe again. In the darkness before the dawn they had sometimes wondered whether England would be catapulted back into the Dark Ages of religious repression. Even now the clemency of the King had been forced by political events. He believed that his throne was in danger from the Puritans and their supporters the Dutch. He relaxed the rules against the Non-Conformists, which included the Roman Catholics on whose support he counted. He did not wish to tolerate the Puritans, but he needed the concrete support of Roman Catholics who had also suffered because of the religious persecution that had imprisoned John.

In order to be released by the Declaration, names of Quakers had to be submitted to the local authorities in the form of a petition. Ironically enough, John's name was included on this list and what became known as 'the Quaker Pardon' was the instrument of John's release, which officially took place on September 13th, 1672, a month after the storm and five months after he had actually left gaol.

He was forty-three, still a strong and healthy man. The strains of living in prison had not weakened his spirit, although it is said that he became sterner as the years went by; twelve years of deprivation had robbed him, a little, of his tenderness and sense of humour.

As the inevitable results of the Declaration of Indulgence became a reality the Bedford congregation turned its attention to the matter of a pastor for their still homeless, but alive, church. Just before John's release the small battered congregation met together in the home of one of their number. They knew that John would soon be free. They needed someone strong and mellow to lead them. They all had stories to tell of their experiences while visiting John, and of how he had eased their hardship in spite of his own. They prayed and discussed at length and then by a show of hands they voted to invite John to become their pastor. It was not a surprising decision, for he had ministered from prison most effectively; now with freedom of movement he was the obvious choice.

John did not become pastor of this small church officially until the day after that terrific storm on August 20th, 1672. In the aftermath of the wind and the rain, in the clean fresh air that follows a storm, he received pastoral responsibility for the small hardy flock that had been as faithful to him as he had to them during the twelve years of persecution and

separation. There is no doubt that some like Merrill and
Deane had fallen by the wayside and John's sternness of
character was quick to condemn those who had turned away
while suffering less than he had been called upon to bear.
John warned his new flock of the consequences of joining
with those who could persecute the Non-Conformists. He
told stories, like that of a man who had spied on the Non-
Conformists and informed on their readings and who died of
a bite which went gangrenous and caused his flesh to drop
off while he repented of his sins. A colleague of this man had
fallen from a steeple and was picked up 'besmeared with
blood', dying horribly. He too had informed on the true
worshippers of God. A third informer had died in agony
cursing the day that Foster had persuaded him to inform.

John was a believer in such stories for this was the style of
the faith of the day, when even the most enlightened men
believed in demons. He allowed these stories to flourish in
the hope that eternal justice did exist on earth. His own
commitment to suffering for the cause made it all the more
necessary to believe that the God who cried, 'Vengeance is
mine, I will repay' was doing just that there and then.
Nevertheless there was much for the Bedford church's pastor
to do and the first thing was to find somewhere for them to
worship. A member of the congregation, Josias Ruffhead,
had bought an orchard from Justice Compton, the very man
who had once out of fear refused bail for John. This orchard
contained a barn and Josias sold it to the congregation for
the sum of fifty pounds. A licence was obtained to use the
barn as a place of worship, and the relaxation of repression
was enough to allow John to preach.

For the first time since the Restoration, the community
could feel real optimism that freedom of religion was on its
way.

The man who had entered Bedford County Gaol twelve
years before was the distinguished pastor of one of the first
Non-Conformist churches in England. His years of prison
had not been a stumbling block to his faith nor to his fame;
on the contrary he was a man of considerable renown, a

controversial theologian and writer. He was so much in demand that all his entries in his diaries for that period are brief. They are full of hurried blots of ink and notes to the effect that he will write up the day's events later. The spaces left for those events were never filled, but there is one incident which from the records of the time, and diaries of someone involved, shows that John's freedom was almost as uncertain as the length of his prison years had been.

14

THE BEAUMONT AFFAIR

November 1672 found John hurrying back from Leicester, where he had been preaching, to Bedford to be present at the birth of his son Joseph. The birth caused no special problems. After their first tragedy Elizabeth had been a proud and capable mother to the children of her own flesh. It was a relief and a joy to both that they were able, at last, to have children, and now a son, of their union. The children of John's first marriage were growing older and more independent, so it was like a new beginning for John when Joseph was born; he hoped sincerely that he would not have to be separated by prison from this son. Joseph was christened in the Anglican Church in 1672. It seemed strange that a minister of a Baptist Church, with a firm belief in adult baptism, should have allowed his son to be christened and certainly that action has provoked vast debate amongst the learned who are puzzled by it. But it is not so unusual when it is realised that christening was also a registering of the birth; that, by law, the two functions took place at the same time. Every child was registered and baptised at the local parish church. John had just spent twelve years in gaol, he was not about to return to it over a ritual that could mean little to him and even less to his son.

November 1672 was to have more significance to John than just the birth of his son, for that was the month in which a young woman, Agnes Beaumont, was accepted into the membership of the Bedford congregation. This was not a particularly important event in itself but was soon to cause problems for John who came to learn of the hazards of fame and freedom.

In the year that followed, Agnes came to adore her pastor and although her faith was not at all false, her adoration was not well disguised. Agnes lived with her widowed father on a small isolated farm between Gamlingay and Hitchin. Her brother and his wife did not attend the Bedford congregation but they were ardent Non-Conformists and had encouraged Agnes in her faith. Her father, however, was different. Originally he too had been interested in the Non-Conformist movement. He had been inspired by his son and daughter-in-law, but Beaumont was neighbour to a rich lawyer named Farrow who had tried to court the elusive Agnes in order to marry her and her inheritance. Farrow, convinced that Non-Conformity was responsible for turning Agnes's heart away from him, set about poisoning the mind of Beaumont against the Puritans. Farrow had been cheated out of a good plot of land by Agnes's dislike of him and her love for John, and he intended to drive her back into his arms if he could not win her love. Agnes's father could see the advantages of a larger farm and resented his daughter's reticence. Agnes, however, ignored both her father and Farrow and continued to attend the Bedford church – until one particular occasion.

In February 1674 a meeting was to be held at Gamlingay, a little way from Bedford and Agnes's home. As the winter was cold and wet, it was impossible for Agnes to get to Gamlingay on foot. She told her brother of her predicament and he arranged that she should come to their farmhouse, just a quarter of a mile away, and there be met by John Wilson, a fellow member of her congregation. She would ride behind him on his horse. The heavy ruts and mud made the going treacherous even for a cart and this was the only solution for the young woman who was desperate not to miss this meeting. Whether Agnes was popular with the congregation was not certain; like many lonely young women, her need for love and friendship was probably only too clear and many disapproved of her attitude towards their pastor. Whatever the reasons, John Wilson did not turn up. They waited hopefully in the cottage for the welcome knock on the door, but it did not come. Agnes's brother and sister-in-law grew more and more concerned that, the way things were going, none of them would get to the meeting. John Beaumont and his wife began to drop hints to her that it might be better if she went home and allowed them to continue on their own. They reassured her that there would be another opportunity for her to join them, but Agnes was growing impatient and would not relieve her brother and sister of their responsibility and suggest that they go on ahead.

At last, when all hope had gone, there came the welcome sound of hooves outside and a knock at the door. John Beaumont, relieved, rushed to the door only to find to his disappointment and Agnes's delight that the rider was John Bunyan. He had called by on an impulse he was soon to regret.

Agnes later wrote her own account of what happened that day and in the weeks after. When she saw the pastor she was overjoyed. Her face gleamed with pleasure at the sight of her beloved John Bunyan, 'but sight of him caused sorrow in me; I was glad to see him, but I was afraid he would not take me to the meeting on his horse'. Agnes was longing to ask him herself but she was consumed by shyness and pulled her brother aside to beg young Beaumont to ask him on her behalf.

The situation was awkward for John, and Agnes had every right to doubt his willingness to carry her. He was not so naive as to think that even the most well-meaning of his congregation would not raise an eyebrow at the sight of a nubile young woman riding pillion behind him. Moreover, he was made more uncomfortable by Agnes's blatant adoration of him; such love should be reserved for a husband or for God, not for a pastor. Despite her innocence she seemed to him a very silly girl, totally unlike the women he had married who bore life and love with strength and resolution. Mary and Elizabeth were restrained in all things, and he could not but dislike this frivolous child. He saw nothing in her he could honour, and worse, as her pastor, he could see no way that he could help her without aggravating the situation. He was gruff in his reply to the request: he did not want to deny her the right to worship but at the same time he could not see how it would help her to carry her. 'No, not me,' he said vehemently. 'I'll not take her.'

Agnes was heartbroken and immediately burst into tears, which caused embarrassment in the family and guilt in John who was not as stern as he sometimes appeared. He was well aware that more than one set of pleading eyes were upon him. Young Beaumont was hoping to avoid a major scene and replied, 'If you don't take her, you will break her heart.' But John renewed his resolution against her. It simply was not possible and a sensible woman would have seen that. He turned to Agnes in the hope of finding some sign of self-restraint and self-sacrifice. 'If I should carry you, your father would be grievous angry with me.' John had obviously met the senior John Beaumont and possibly his neighbour Farrow. He knew well man's ability to sin: he had felt it in his own heart, and had been a victim of the spite of the authorities in gaol. He saw the danger of it here. However Agnes would not show that timidity that John hoped for and perhaps a little unfairly expected of the lonely young woman. She assured him that she would answer to her father. 'If you please carry me,' she pleaded. 'I'll deal with him.'

John could resist no longer. How could he deny someone the right to worship with her fellow Christians just because she had been let down by someone else? Reluctantly he allowed her to climb up behind him and ride pillion on his horse. Agnes was overjoyed; not only was she going to the meeting, but she was going in the company of her beloved pastor. She eagerly clung to her saviour. 'My heart was lifted up and riding behind this servant of the Lord, I was so pleased if any even looked at us as we passed.' While Agnes was pleased that people noticed them John cringed with embarrassment and foreboding. Agnes made the most of her ride, and revelled in the notoriety that it brought her. John, by now well known as a somewhat austere man, must have caused some surprise when the young woman was spotted on his horse behind him. In Agnes's father the sight evoked an evil rage, for he saw them in the distance and rushed to a crossroads to try and drag his daughter from the horse, but he arrived too late and he could only stand in apoplectic fury to wait for her return.

Had John seen Agnes's father he might have had some justification in asking her to dismount. It would have been just the excuse he needed, but as it was, they rode together into Gamlingay, unaware of the fury behind them. Agnes was hardly restrained next to John and many an interested tongue began to wag in speculation. John was forty-five, getting to that age when a man seeks his lost youth and, in John's case, his wasted years. John was very anxious that Agnes should behave with some propriety, but one look at her ecstatic face at the meeting provoked even more speculation amongst the congregation. 'How willingly I would have died in that place and gone to glory,' she said. Better that than face the walk home in the cold and dark, for John was in no mood to take her back, and no one else offered. At last another young woman was found who lived quite near Agnes's home and it was arranged that they should walk together; at least for six of the seven miles Agnes would have company.

Agnes did not get back home until very late that night, a fact which aggravated her already overwrought father, for when she returned wet and cold she found the door of her home bolted against her. 'It's me, father, come home all wet and dirty. Please let me in.' At first Agnes was too overwhelmed by the evening to be perturbed by her father's behaviour but from behind the door an angered voice called, 'Where you have been all day, there you may go at night.' Beaumont senior had had hours to think about what may have happened to Agnes with John Bunyan on the road to Gamlingay and more particularly on the long journey back. Agnes stood below the window where her father had now stationed himself, pleading with him and crying. She was cold and miserable, the warmth of the fellowship and the evening now seemed a long way away and the price she was being asked to pay for such fellowship was very high. At last, enraged and pained by his daughter's pleas, Beaumont threatened to run her off the property if she did not leave him alone. Miserable and disappointed, Agnes retreated to the barn in the hope that the morning would bring a more reasonable temper to her father.

It crossed her mind to go back to her brother's home, but she had already faced that walk alone through the fields once that night and she did not fancy it again. After that slight hesitation she continued to the barn, where, cold and desperate, she began to reflect on her position. Perhaps she had committed some great sin, perhaps her attitude was more extreme than she could feel. Did she commit, in her heart, the sin of fornication with John? Surely not, but she was uncertain. Did she deserve all that was happening to her? She tried to remember as many scriptural phrases as she could. Voices in her head called to her, much as they had done to John when he had travailed in his dark night. 'Beloved, think it not strange concerning the fiery trial which is coming.' Agnes was ecstatic at this sentence, which she heard as clearly as if someone stood with her in the barn. Like John who heard the Devil at his side, or the voice of God reprimanding him, Agnes, too, heard these supernatural voices and may well have been influenced by the stories she heard told by John at the meetings. Agnes worshipped and praised; she had heard the voice of God and He had called her 'beloved'.

'It was a blessed night,' she recalls, 'never to be forgotten. Oh, the near ravishing visits He gave me.' Agnes approached even her prayers in a fever of devotion and all that night she knelt in prayer, asking God not to cast her out on the Last Day as her father had done, but to witness to her faithfulness in the face of opposition.

The next morning found her shivering and still damp, trying to persuade a no less adamant father to let her in. 'Good morning to you, father, I've had a cold night's lodging here, but God has been good to me.' Her words were not calculated to soothe him, but were rather a provocation.

'And so?' replied her father.

She pleaded with him again, to let her in, but he would not
be moved. 'Father,' she admonished. 'Can you stand in my
stead and answer for me on Judgment Day? If so I will obey
you in this as in all other things.'

But Beaumont insisted that the only condition under
which he would let her back would be if she gave up going to
the Puritan meetings. Agnes continued to plead with him
until the farm workers arrived. Some of them were her
brother's men and were shocked at what they found: Agnes,
cold and wet and clearly in a highly emotional state, her
father in a murderous rage.

They hurried back to tell young John Beaumont of their
discovery. He ran up to the farm to plead with his father on
Agnes's behalf, but the old man remained implacable. Either
she give up the meetings or she leave his land. At last, Agnes
retreated with her brother to his home, bedraggled and
tearful but believing herself to be suffering for the work of
the Lord. The old man's rage followed them down the hill as
they walked sorrowfully away. The last threat of such a man
was bellowed at their presented backs; he would leave
nothing to her in his will. 'Not a penny!' he screamed. 'Not a
penny!'

Agnes spent the week assaulted by fear. What if she had to
work for a living? Go into service? It would be hard for her
who had always served only those whom she loved, and had
been looked after by them rather than paid in return. Her
brother tried to reassure her, but the consequences of living
away from her father were too much to bear and one evening
she crept back to try again.

When she reached the familiar farmhouse she found that
the door had been left ajar, with the key in it. Thanking God
for his mercy and taking this as a sign that the Lord wished
her to return, she grabbed the key and ran away. She rushed
to the pond and there stood willing herself to fling it in and
thus ensure herself of entrance back into the cottage. Her
father, however, had not been far away, and he caught up
with her by the pond and shook and hit her. 'Hussy!' he

screamed. 'Give me that key or I will throw you into the pond.' She returned the key and ran away, crying.

Shaken by her father's violence she lost all hope.

'Call upon me,' she heard suddenly, above the sound of her own tears. It was that voice again, the one that had comforted her in the barn. 'Call upon me and I will answer thee.' Agnes stayed where she was, in the woods between the two cottages. There she waited expecting something – she did not know what – but perhaps hoping that God would come and take her.

She was not found until her brother, aware that she was missing, sent out a search party. Again cold and sad, Agnes was brought to her brother's cottage. There he persuaded her that she had no choice but to stand up to her father; if she did so, then no matter what happened she would be a martyr to God's cause, and she could claim a martyr's crown. She was indeed blessed.

So she went once more to her father, at her brother's direction, but this time she went to tell him that she would rather beg in the street than submit to his will. The next day, she and her brother and her sister-in-law felt that she should stay away from the meeting that Sunday, in order to allow some hope of continued negotiations. Agnes spent a lonely Sunday then, away from the fellowship for which she had sacrificed so much and separated from her beloved John Bunyan. Bored and restless, she went once more to the house to try and reach some kind of compromise, but still the old man would not listen. 'Father, I will serve you in anything that lies in my power, I only desire liberty to hear God's word.'

'If you promise,' old Beaumont began again, 'never to go to a meeting as long as I'm alive you shall never leave this house and I will provide for you as my own child.'

'Father, my soul is worth more than that.'

'Then go, but if you promise, I will give you the key,' he held the key out towards her.

Agnes gazed at it. If she took it then the life of hardship and poverty that threatened her would be averted. Yet if she took it, the eternal damnation of her soul would lie in its wake.

'If you refuse it now you shall never be offered it again. What do you say, hussy? Will you promise or not?'

The choice was a terrible one. Agnes needed her father and her will was hardly strong enough for this; even the voices that had comforted her and the insistence of her brother could not help her now. She gave in and took the key. She agreed never to go to a meeting again. She would never see her adored John Bunyan again.

Her father, although harsh, was not a vindictive man and he was forgiving in his triumph. He was affectionate immediately, glowing in the loyalty and love of his daughter. But Agnes found no rest in what she had done. She was quiet and miserable, despite her father's attempts to cheer her. She believed she had damned her soul to hell. In the night she dreamed of an old apple tree that fell and no matter what she did she could not lift it. On Monday, still uncertain, she prayed, 'Oh Lord, Lord what shall I do?' and she heard again the voice. 'There shall be a way of escape that you may be able to bear it.'

That night after supper Agnes cried desperately, no longer able to hide her grief from her father, no longer able to assure him that she had denied her faith with a glad heart, convinced of his rightness. Her father tried to find out what troubled her, but she would only tell him that she was hurt because of the promise she had made. Moved to compassion by his daughter's tears, hurt perhaps by the knowledge that it was his cruelty that caused her misery, the old man fell to his knees and also wept. He too had once been moved by the preaching of John Bunyan, he too had once been fired by the Puritan cause, but he was a simple man and his mind was easily turned, he believed the educated Mr Farrow and his malicious intent towards Puritans. Surely if such an educated man thought they were evil, then they were so, and he could not but keep his daughter away, if he was to serve her as a father should. Nevertheless the old curiosity and the old Puritan flame still smouldered. Beaumont was a confused man. He confessed to his daughter his feelings and even said that his reaction to her riding behind John Bunyan may have been over harsh, but still he held her to her promise, believing that to be his duty as her father. The weary couple wept together and then Agnes helped her father to bed; it was a Tuesday night and, as she laid him down, the voice came again: 'The end is come.'

She went to bed, puzzled by the message, but she slept for a while, exhausted by the day's emotions. She woke at the sound of strange noises coming from her father's room. The strain and high emotions of the past weeks had taken their toll. 'How long have you been ill?' She stood aghast at the foot of her father's bed, horrified by the pain on his face, while her candle threw its light on his racked features.

'I was struck with a pain at my heart in my sleep,' he gasped, every word a moan, 'and shall die presently.'

Agnes knelt at the bedside, trying to ease her father's agony. He sobbed and fought against the attack. Seeing that she could not help him she begged him to let her go for help, but he could not bear to let her out of his sight.

'Oh, I want mercy for my soul, I have been against you for seeking after Jesus Christ, the Lord forgive me!' His anguish tore at her heart and she tried to reassure her father of God's love, but he would not take comfort. He started to get up and put on his clothes. Agnes, unable to persuade him to lie down again, helped him as best she could, thinking she could perhaps drag him across the fields to some help.

Once downstairs she made up the fire in the hope that warmth would soothe him but he grew worse; he retched violently and gasped for air, he would not sit still. His face began to blacken and contort. She was, by now, terrified, wondering if her father were not just ill but possessed by some terrible demon. She could not get him to sit down, she had to prop him against herself for he was in serious danger of falling into the fire.

'Lord,' he cried, 'spare me one week more, one day more.' He called for a candle for he said it was dark around him. He wanted to get to the other room away from the fire, it seemed

like hell. He made as if to go there, but the stroke took him
and his back arched and his fingers strove silently against the
air. He tried to hold himself up but the effort was useless and
he fell. Agnes screamed and attempted to lift him but it was
no use; she could not even make him more comfortable.
Terrified of the evil of the night Agnes hesitated over what to
do, but she perceived that her father was still alive and there
might still be hope. His black face, tormented by the pain,
pleaded with her silently not to go, but more afraid of him
than of the night, she fled into the darkness through the
newly-fallen snow to hammer hysterically on her brother's
door.

Her brother and two men hurried to the house where they
found Beaumont no longer conscious but still alive. They
carried him up to the bedroom and ordered Agnes to wait
outside. Agnes, already seeing the Hand of God that released
her from her promises, prayed, a little callously perhaps, that
his soul should find its sleep in eternity by midnight, and it
did.

The following day, one of the first neighbours to reach
their farmhouse was the covetous Mr Farrow, still hoping
that Beaumont's property might come his way. On seeing
Agnes he marched up to her and asked, 'Is your father dead?'

'Yes,' replied Agnes, looking for signs of grief and
sympathy on Farrow's face.

Instead he said, 'It is no more than I looked for.' He turned
away with nothing more to say to her, but preparing an
attack.

15

ACCUSATIONS AND DENIALS

The news of old Beaumont's death found its way to the Baldock fair and many people remembered that John Bunyan had ridden into Gamlingay with Agnes Beaumont at his back. Farrow had not forgotten the incident either, and, the day before the funeral, he began his opening moves. He approached the young and grieving John Beaumont and asked him whether he had any suspicion that his father had not died naturally.

'No,' said John, 'I know he did.' He was well aware of Farrow's reputation and had no liking for him or his words.

'But,' said Farrow, weighing the effect of his words, 'I believe he did not, and I have had my horse out of the stable twice today to fetch a surgeon.' He paused as if out of respect. 'But I considered that you are an officer of the parish, therefore I leave the matter to you.' Young Beaumont knew full well that the matter was not left to him; Farrow was sly and the threat of exposure was there, for if Beaumont did nothing himself, Farrow would soon force the issue and state his accusations publicly. If that happened it would look worse for the family.

'Pray,' said Farrow, underlining his point, 'and see you do your office... I believe your sister has poisoned him!'

John Beaumont took seriously what was said, if only because he knew what Farrow would do if he was ignored and that would look worse for them all. He consulted with a friend who advised him that Agnes should be told of the accusation and an investigation should be ordered. The funeral was postponed and Agnes held herself tense. She was

convinced of the justice of the law and was clear in her own
conscience.

A surgeon was called in to conduct a post-mortem. He
questioned her severely: what had they done that evening?
Had they argued? What had he eaten? Had she prepared the
food? The examination complete, the surgeon took the
matter into his own hands and went to Farrow himself to tell
him that he saw no grounds for suspicion. Farrow, however,
would not be convinced. He was committed to the
accusation and his own reputation was at stake. Reluctantly
the surgeon informed the Beaumonts that the coroner
should be called in for now only the court could proclaim
Agnes's innocence. Again the voice comforted Agnes. 'No
weapon that is fired against thee shall prosper!'

Nevertheless she was frightened, for she was on trial for
her life at a time when the haunting trials for witchcraft
could still claim a victim. The punishment for Agnes would
be burning at the stake and she wondered whether she could
bear it. She faced it as a real possibility and the flames
seemed sometimes to lick at her feet. Farrow's reputation,
however, was well known and before Agnes stood trial, most
of the jury assured her of their belief in her innocence. Still
comforted by the voices in her mind, convinced that even if
she should burn God would be with her, she protested her
innocence to the court. She found the Judge's attitude to her
rather stern at first and she thought that he did not like her,
but he was even more severe with her accuser, the lawyer
Farrow. As a lawyer he should have known what kind of
evidence would constitute a charge, but all he could do was
bring accusations, insinuations and no firm evidence and
the Judge insisted that he must bring proof of motivate.
Farrow pointed to John Bunyan and said that Agnes had
conspired with him to kill the old man for they had later
planned to marry (having dispensed with John's wife
presumably).

After a second interrogation of Agnes in which the Judge
called her a 'sweetheart', he gave Farrow the verdict. 'You,
sir, who have defamed this young woman in this public

manner, endeavouring to take away her good name and her life as well, if you could, ought to make it your business now to establish her good reputation!' He told Farrow that Agnes had suffered quite enough and if Farrow were to pay her five hundred pounds it would not compensate for his cruelty towards her. To Agnes he said, 'Sweetheart, don't be daunted, God will take care of you and provide you with a husband, notwithstanding the malice of this man.'

But Farrow's malice was not quite spent. He had gone to some trouble to persuade old Beaumont to leave his property to Agnes so that he could acquire it by marrying her. Now he could not bear to see her enjoying the fruits of his deviousness. He sent for her brother-in-law from the graveside at the funeral and told him that he would act on behalf of his wife, Agnes's sister, to contest the will and get back some of the property left to Agnes. Agnes, however, had pre-empted him. She made a handsome gift to her sister out of the estate and that settled that!

Nevertheless, despite all her efforts to clear her name, it was still rumoured and believed by many that she had confessed to a conspiracy with John Bunyan and poisoned her father. In Biggleswade market they talked of little else, so much so that to prove her good name, Agnes went to Biggleswade and, in the market square, she announced to them all that she had never conspired with anyone to kill her father, let alone with John Bunyan. But her actions were not enough. Still, the people talked, always willing to believe the worst of someone, especially someone who was supposed to be pious. John himself found that his good reputation and years of martyrdom were not sufficient to protect him from the mudslinging. After all his suffering for a worthy cause, the years in gaol and the proof of piety, people still insisted that there was no smoke without fire. John was forced to defend himself and said so in the later editions of his autobiography, *Grace Abounding to the Chief of Sinners*. The slander existed and it must be refuted. 'Then he [Satan]' says John, 'tried another way in which to stir up the minds of the ignorant, and their malicious reproaches, now therefore

I may say that what the Devil could devise and his instruments invent was whirled up and down the county against me, thinking, as I said by that means they should make an end to my ministry.'

John had encountered evil before, threatening to his existence, but now he encountered the evil of men's minds. He challenged his slanderers to present their lies to God on Judgment Day, for the revelation of the Truth would increase his glory as a martyr: 'Therefore I bind these lies and slanders to me, as an ornament it belongs to my Christian profession to be fulfilled... I rejoice in reproaches for Christ's sake.'

John denied most vehemently that he had carnally known any woman other than his wives, and he defiantly challenged the public that if all the adulterers, fornicators and liars were to be hung by the neck until dead, he, John Bunyan, would outlive them all and more.

16

PRISON AND THE PILGRIM

John's freedom had been a stormy affair and no sooner had the memory of Agnes begun to fade in the public mind, than an old threat returned to hunt John down. There was a new move to crush dissent in the country; the King had become a puppet of the Anglican clergy, who feared a Papal invasion. At least this was so on the surface, but secretly the King sought a way to return England to the Papal fold. He negotiated with Louis XIV of France to bring about an alliance with Catholic France. So while harsh laws were revived and instituted to stamp out Non-Conformity, Protestant and Catholic, the King conspired to bring England closer to Rome. Internally the squires and middle-classes defied the new repression and the King had to move against them. Now, in 1675, the oppression that overtook the country began again to threaten John. The Bedford Church's licence was revoked, the brief period of sunlight was over and a new darkness overtook the Church. John was once again an outlaw.

A colleague came to his house, a brother who knew the mind of old William Foster and who warned John that there was another warrant out for his arrest. The warrant carried the signatures of thirteen Magistrates. Foster was the force behind this warrant, for he was still determined to halt the activities of 'Bishop' Bunyan. The Conventicle Acts were re-enforced and withdrew the licences of preachers such as John. Foster was sure that this time he could get him now that the penalties were more damaging. A twenty-pound fine for the first offence and a forty-pound fine for the second, then all the possessions of the culprit to be sold leaving him and his family destitute; then and only then, would the culprit go to gaol, leaving his family beggared and with no means of support. Such a harsh punishment would be a disaster for Elizabeth and their still-young children: Joseph was only two years old. John therefore reluctantly took heed of the warning and retreated to the road. He had to get out of the jurisdiction of Bedford County. In effect he was banished.

For eighteen months John travelled between his friends, Luke Ashwood at Gamlingay, John Wilson at Hitchin and John Gibbs at Newport Pagnell. Once again he was separated from his family, for Elizabeth could not travel easily with the children, so he had to love even his younger children, the children of his second marriage, from a distance, unable to share in their everyday growth. He never would know now the true joy of fatherhood, the day-to-day living with a growing loving child. He was forced to snatch his moments with them when he could, like a starving man snatches food, never able to feel satisfied, always wondering if there would be more. But the pressure and the novelty of freedom had brought back his inspiration and he wrote three further, rather heavy, theological treatises. A simple tinker he may have been, but to William Foster's fury he managed to outwit the authorities and use his pen as effectively as ever.

Two or three years earlier, John's name had been presented to the vicar and churchwarden of St Cuthbert's in Bedford for refusing to go to church regularly and take Communion. John was excommunicated. That was a normal occurrence for many Non-Conformists although, in the accepted codes of his society, it meant that he was damned to hell. John did not believe this, but neither did he realise the full significance of this move. At night, when he doubted, he may have feared hell once more, but the fact that his name was forwarded to Chancery for a 'signification of excommunication' was more immediately serious, for it made his criminality national. He was vulnerable, wherever he went, to arrest.

John was a little complacent about the writ that Chancery had issued, perhaps because he knew that re-arrest was inevitable whatever he did, or perhaps because he did not know the power of the writ. He realised that the Anglicans were frustrated by their helplessness and that ultimately they would move against him. Ordinary communication was not easy then and it was eighteen months after the issue of the warrant by Foster that John was finally arrested and taken back to Bedford gaol.

Although his prison sentence was not to be nearly as long as the twelve years of the last term, John was not to know that, and he fought a very desperate misery as the doors closed behind him. How long would it be this time? Could he bear another twelve years? Would it end in death? The gallows? Would Elizabeth manage? Was this the beginning of an even more severe period of persecution? The old fears fluttered round his cell on the wings of these demons of terror. John tossed and turned in a wakeful sleep. He was older now, his bones ached the quicker and he slept less well. He was more vulnerable to colds and fever; would he be able physically to stand up to the rigours of prison life as well as he did the last time? He was again tempted to give up and let go, but he had already suffered so much he could not neglect his journey now.

He lay in his cell sometimes crying silently to himself when he could not be observed. It did not get easier as he got older. He loved Elizabeth more than ever and he longed for his children and grieved for his poor blind Mary who struggled so bravely, and missed him so desperately. He longed too for relief from the responsibility that forced him to go on being a figure-head, a martyr, a leader of the Puritans. He wanted God to find someone else, or to take him 'home'. He yearned for it all to end, to be resolved one way or another. The thought of twelve more years in gaol made him sick and cold and he shivered, trying not cry out. In twelve years he would be an old man.

For the first few weeks he found some solace in sleep, he hid from the boredom and discomfort in dreams of the

countryside and freedom. In his fitful half waking, half
sleeping state a figure began to form in his mind: a man with
a heavy, almost unbearable burden on his back like the
portable anvil of his trade. The figure set out from his home,
waving goodbye to his wife and family. He began walking
country lanes similar to those of Elstow and Bedford. He
was jaunty but perhaps over-confident and as such he began
laboriously and painfully to climb a hill. The burden almost
pulled him over and John feared that the figure would never
reach the top of the hill, he was so hindered by the weight of
his burden. It seemed he could not bear it, and then John saw
that at the summit was a cross, a stark and impelling image
that drew the figure on, until at last he could kneel at its feet
and pray. Immediately the burden fell away rolling back
down the hill. The figure sprang up, as light on his feet as if
he himself had no weight at all, he leapt for joy at the relief
and began to sing. As he did so he turned to face the watcher,
the dreamer, and John, with a shock, saw that the figure was
himself. He awoke uncertain of the meaning of what he had
just seen, and thus began the famous story of *The Pilgrim's
Progress*. John was already a famous man, but this was to be
his most spectacular success.

John became obsessed by the dream. His waking hours
were filled with its images, he could not shake it off, it
exhausted him. So he wrote it down but all the same he could
not deny the feeling that to do so was to indulge himself in a
very frivolous way. It was unlike anything ever written
before, a totally original work, and John had nothing to
judge it by. Was he being distracted by this story from his
real and more important theological works? Was the Devil
drawing him away from the truth? He could not believe that
this was so, for the dream seemed compellingly true,
powerful in communicating the Christian journey. He
pressed on in faith.

John's pilgrim faced as much fear and danger as he had
himself. He ploughed through the Slough of Despond. He
was captured and imprisoned by the Giant Despair. He
walked through the valley of the Shadow of Death. The

story was full of heroic imagery, like that associated with the knights and dragons of the legends of King Arthur. It was an epic work, like Milton's *Paradise Lost,* but it was lighter than that, it had a more common appeal; it heralded the great tradition of English novel writing; it was certainly the forerunner of the fictional narrative method.

Pilgrim appealed to a society that feared demons and had witnessed the hypocrisy of the worshippers who gained salvation through infant baptism. Those Puritans and Quakers (even Catholics), of faith who had suffered for their loyalty and fidelity, recognised the characters of 'Worldly Wiseman' who always knew better (or so he thought) 'Pliable' and 'Talkative' whose names were self-explanatory and simple but whose faithlessness and constant seeking after the easy way to the Celestial City discouraged the conscientious Christian. It portrayed the traitors who had informed on the people of God, it illustrated clearly and comically the way those who were faithless appeared at first to prosper but never reached the Celestial City. It tapped the sense of humour of the age, its readers laughed at the antics of the foolish and revelled in the satisfactory demise of the evil and they cheered on the faithful who did reach their reward. It encouraged those who suffered for the faith and could only hope for reward.

The book appealed to the most basic instincts of the reader: the poor man who suffered but remained good constantly watched the evil man prosper from his deviousness and perversion, but *Pilgrim's Progress* reflected a greater truth than worldly values, and the reader knew that, whatever their apparent success, the evil would get their just reward and the good, however humble, would be recognised and received into eternal happiness. The caricatures were funny pantomine figures and the story, although moralistic, was tense. The readers wanted to tell Christian not to trust the side path, not to believe in his dubious companions. The readers were led by John to know where the straight and narrow path lay, but were kept in suspense when Christian departed from it and suffered disaster. Would he get out of it in the end? Christian, to the relief of all who read it, survived to an exultant eternity. As an allegory of death alone, it soothed the fears of many.

Pilgrim's Progress must have been as satisfying to John to write as it was to many to read. 'As I walked through the wilderness of this world, I lighted on a certain place, where was a den.' The den was his prison, his life was sometimes a wilderness. John describes how he lay down in his den and slept. He dreamt of a better world, as men do who suffer the evil of this one. It soothed him to write the story as it purged his misery, although he often wondered whether it was not a self-indulgent release, for in describing the lanes and countryside of Christian's journey, he described the countryside of Elstow and Bedford, the places and roads he had walked when free. Elstow church tower and its North East portal have been cited as the 'Tower of Beelzebul', and the Wicket Gate through which Christian first walks from the City of Destruction could be seen from John's Elstow home. The Valley of the Shadow of Death bears a remarkable resemblance to a local gorge, and many other places that John once visited he visualised now, in gaol, as he wrote his epic tale.

When it was finished, John, uncertain as to whether it had any merit, decided to try it out on his fellow prisoners. It seemed as good a way as any to fill the long evenings. Among his fellows were the ordinary felons who might benefit from it and, of course, other Non-Conformists, harsher critics. John read with the humour he hoped would lighten the moral tale. The men listened quietly, unaware that they were receiving a unique preview, and not all recognised it as the classic it was soon to become. John finished the last sentence with a nervous apprehension, which he had not really experienced before when presenting his work. He felt very vulnerable. He put the manuscript down hopefully and waited for the verdict of his friends. His heart beat a little faster; this austere and famous man was now, more than ever before, at the mercy of his critics. Had they merely listened politely? Did they understand it? Were they now searching for gentle words with which to break the news of his failure? Had they been caught up by it?

He broke the silence, ready for whatever they had to say. 'Well, should I print it?'

'Yes,' said some.

'No,' said others.

An impasse, or so it seemed. No one appeared to have hated it or not to have understood it, but it was just so new, they were, like him, unsure of its doctrine, or whether doctrine should be expressed in such a way. The discussion continued for some time; it had certainly livened up the prison.

Amongst those who considered the case was a young man, later to become pastor of a church in Luton. He asked John if he might read it again by himself. Like others, Thomas thought that it reduced religion to the level of cheap romance, but he wanted another look at it before he condemned such a distinguished fellow prisoner. John gave him the manuscript, glad to be rid of it and its puzzling obsession for a while.

Thomas read it again and returned to John with a changed mind.

'Yes,' he advised John. 'Print it.'

So, when the book was published, John provided a little explanation at the beginning about the discussion that had led to its publication.

> Some said 'John print it' others said 'no'
> Some said 'it might do good' others said 'no'
> Now I was in a straight and did not see
> Which was the best thing to be done by me
> At last I thought, since you are thus divided
> I print it will, and so the case decided.

17

THE CELESTIAL CITY

John had spent twenty years defying the authorities. He had never committed a crime to banish him or hang him. Now as he sat alone in gaol, waiting, wondering, writing, he received the news that his father had died. Thomas Bunyan had never joined his son's congregation and John never really forgave him for marrying so soon after his mother's death. Whatever the feelings between the two men it was a hard blow, for John was unable to go to the old man's bedside and offer a few tender words of farewell and understanding. He was unable to say the things that he had never had time to say. John was left alone, ever wondering whether his father was proud of his gaoled son or disappointed in him, and it was hard to accept that the old man had died not knowing whether John would ever regain his freedom. Nevertheless over the years he had grown consistently more famous and therefore more difficult to punish. The authorities were weary and so when in June 1677 two Non-Conformist ministers drew up a bond and offered a surety that John would conform to the Establishment within six months, the move was welcomed with relief. Nobody was under any illusion that John would conform or recant at all, let alone within six months; they merely hoped that he would not push things beyond the limits of a certain toleration. There was a silent agreement to turn a blind eye. After all the sureties were being offered by fellow Non-Conformists who wanted him free but unchanged.

So John was released, never again to be imprisoned. His family could once again welcome him home. Mary was a grown woman now, and, despite her blindness, she was a real help to Elizabeth with the younger children. The boys were boisterous teenagers with an energy level that John could no longer match and Elizabeth, despite the hardships of the years, was still a youthful and good-humoured mother to all the children, who cherished her as they now cherished their spiritually battered father.

For John the novelty of being free once more was both a relief and a reminder of his wasted years. He found that he was superfluous to his family's needs. Almost inevitably they had grown apart, and John was restless. He wanted a change of scene and when the opportunity for a trip to London to supervise the publication of *Pilgrim's Progress* arose, he took it. Matthias Cowley, his old supporter and the previous distributor of his books, had died in the previous year, so Nathanial Ponder was to publish *Pilgrim's Progress*. It was registered at the Stationer's Hall, on December 22nd, 1677 and licensed on February 18th, 1678. It was published in a small pocketbook version, twenty-six pages long, and it cost one shilling and sixpence. By the time John died in 1688 it had been reprinted eleven times and one hundred thousand copies were sold in just eleven years. It was a magnificent best-seller which kept Nathanial Ponder's printing works busy for life, so much so that Nathanial earned the nickname, 'Bunyan's Ponder'. The demand was so great and encouraging that John added a few more characters like Mr By Ends and Mr Worldly Wiseman in the later editions.

However, in those early days of February and March 1678, while John and Nathanial prepared to publish the book, they were not even half aware of the fame it would bring them. In those busy days John took time off to do a little sightseeing, to look at the city and exercise his newly recovered freedom. London was rising from its ashes, a new and modern London, but everywhere there was still evidence of the Fire. The extent of the destruction was greater than John had ever imagined, despite the tales he had heard of it. Now, though, there were the first signs of recovery, with St Paul's just beginning to rise from the ruins. London had crossed the frontier from the Middle Ages and was now a vast and busy commercial port, full of life and business. It was not the austere Puritan city that John had once known; theatres, clubs and inns flourished and the Stuarts were outrageous in their behaviour and dress. The dark restrictions of Oliver Cromwell had caused a backlash under Charles II. Men wore long curly wigs which stretched down their backs, puffed blouses and frills, rings; they took snuff, which John abhorred; they carried scented handkerchiefs, but perhaps the worst of all for John was the make up, the powdered lead used to make their faces white, the beauty spots and the coloured lips that made the men imitate the women in looks and actions. A moralistic tale such as *Pilgrim's Progress* was much needed.

Not everything in London had suffered in the Fire; a certain Pinner's Hall, built by the Pinmaker's Company in 1635, was let after the Restoration to a group of Independents. It became a famous institution and began an event called the 'Merchant's Lecture'. It survived only twenty-two years after John's second release, but there he was to preach one of his greatest sermons, 'The Greatness of the Soul', which was later printed.

The unforeseen success of *Pilgrim's Progress* took John by surprise but he was not at a loss; having once discovered a new and useful form of literature, he was inspired to write more such stories. Allegories, it seems, were a form that came easily to him, for in the years that followed, as well as preaching, travelling and ministering to his own congregation, John followed up Pilgrim's story with a sequel about Christiana, Christian's wife. Then came *The Holy War*, about the siege of the town of Mansoul by the forces of evil and good. There was *The Life and Death of Mr Badman* which took the form of a conversation between two people, much like the book that had first influenced John all those years ago, *The Plain Man's Pathway to Heaven*, which had been a conversation between four people.

It is possible that in writing *The Life and Death of Mr Badman* John had someone specific in mind; even though the scandal of Agnes Beaumont had faded, John was not without his slanderers now. Amongst his congregation was a man who by his behaviour appeared mentally unbalanced. He was called Mr Wildman and his name denoted his behaviour. In 1680, for no apparent reason, this man accused John of fiddling the Church finances. The Church turned on Wildman and warned him that if he did not repent he would be ostracised. Wildman was silenced but he still grumbled and the tension remained. John hated divisions and the presence of the vindictive Mr Wildman meant that the Church which he so dearly loved was no longer a haven of fellowship, encouraging him and his family, but a place of constant strife. John had grown intolerant of such behaviour after the years of loneliness in prison and a haunted freedom. He sought his own company now voluntarily, when once it been forced on him. Whenever he could he found an excuse to absent himself, sometimes for very long periods.

In 1683 a Church meeting was held to discuss Wildman's case, for he had not stopped his accusations, and John had at last decided to try to dismiss him. Although he was ostracised, Wildman never gave up; he was still trying to get back into the Church in 1699, eleven years after John's death.

John was by now very famous. Towards the end of his life Charles Doe (an early biographer and friend) recalls that even if only one day's notice was given that John was to preach in the City of London, so many people would attend that they would not all have room to hear. John would not have been able to hide so easily as before if intolerance were to recur.

The situation did revert to instability once more before the law finally eased. In the late 1670s, Titus Oates had rocked the country by claiming to have infiltrated the Jesuits and discovered a conspiracy to kill the King; in 1683 the Rye House Plot to assassinate the King was discovered. John feared that in another clamp-down he might be taken once more to finish his days in gaol. He made a will.

Know ye that I, the said John Bunyan, as well as far and in

consideration of the natural affection and love which I
have and bear unto my well-loved wife, Elizabeth Bunyan,
as so for divers other good causes, and consideration
are at this present especially... all singular my goods,
chattels, debts, ready money, plate and all my other good
substance.

John had it witnessed and sealed it then he hid it, but only
too well, for it was not found until 1838 when his house was
pulled down. Poor Elizabeth had to manage as the widow of
an intestate.

John had been justified in his fear, for the Rye House Plot
brought much suffering on many Non-Conformists, al-
though the process was interrupted by the death of Charles
II. James II was no better. He too was sympathetic to the
Roman Catholic Church and was convinced that the
Anglican Church could be persuaded back into the arms of
Rome because of its vicious opposition to the Puritans.
Parliament however remained implacably both anti-
Catholic and anti-Puritan; rebels were brought to the
scaffold by the notorious Judge Jeffreys in what was later to
be called the Bloody Assize, but paradoxically England
received and sheltered the fleeing Non-Conformists of the
Continent, the Huguenots.

The Bloody Assize was an insult to human rights, and
even in those days the English public was outraged by such
atrocities. Moreover it escaped few people's notice that the
King had provided himself with considerable powers of
repression. In defiance, Franciscan monks paraded openly
in the streets and public Mass was celebrated. As a result
there were riots. James II, impressed by the strength of
feeling, issued another Declaration of Indulgence and lifted
all the restrictions on both Catholics and Puritans. The
Anglican Church was alarmed by this and now sought the
support of the Puritan movement to combat the Roman
Catholics, but John, like many others, refused to allow
himself to be used as a puppet for the Church's anti-Catholic
policy. He would not team up with those who had denied

him over thirteen years of freedom.

Passions rose and the intrigue increased and before 1688 was over the Dutch Prince, William of Orange, had landed at Torbay and James II had fled before him. England became a free Protestant country.

That promised land, though, was one that John could only see from afar. He never lived to know that his people could always be free to worship without persecution.

Religious restrictions were nevertheless easier in his last years than they had been. Judge Jeffreys and his Bloody Assize had frightened and enraged, but the general atmosphere was more tolerant. John travelled a great deal in his fiftieth decade for, after years of being kept in one place, he shifted restlessly from town to town. Charles Doe said of him, 'When he was at leisure from writing and teaching he often came up to London, and there went among the congregations of Non-Conformists and used his talents to the great good-liking of his hearers.' As a famous and much-loved man he was in demand both by congregations and individuals and his service to them was to cost him dear, for he could never refuse an appeal for help.

One particular feud between father and son had festered, so John was asked to intervene on behalf of the son to try to end the impasse. The son was a neighbour of John's but unfortunately the father lived further afield in Reading. John decided to divert to Reading en route to a preaching appointment in London. When he arrived he found the father very open to what he had to say and the way was well prepared for the son to follow. The journey had hardly been necessary. John mounted his horse in Reading. He carried with him his last manuscript, *The Excellency of Broken Heart*, which he was taking to Nathanial Ponder.

When John left Reading it was raining and as he continued the conditions got worse. It began to pour and he rode the forty miles to John Strudwick's house in London in the raging weather. He looked an old and bedraggled sight when he finally knocked on his friend's door later that night. They hurried him in, changed his clothes, sat him by the fire

and provided hot drinks and food. They fussed over him,
watching for signs of ill health, but when nothing but a slight
cold showed they were relieved, and John decided that he
was well enough to preach the following day.

That Sunday he preached at Whitechapel, suffering a little
from the effects of the journey and a nasty cough that caught
in his throat. On the Tuesday, what had been a troublesome
cold turned into a fever. Fevers were common and John had
often suffered them in gaol, so his hosts reasoned he was
toughened and able to withstand this one. The alarm was
not raised, and no message was sent to Elizabeth. But the
fever grew worse and John suffered violent shaking and
convulsions. The cough hacked at him and he became
delirious. He had pneumonia. The Strudwicks grew more
and more afraid; nothing they could do seemed to stop the
inevitable march of death. They could only watch as their
treasured guest commenced his journey across the river
about which he had once written so brilliantly.

In his more lucid moments he comforted his frantic
friends. He claimed that he was looking forward to his death,
counting it as a marvellous gain. He suffered bravely but
wearily. He had given up the fight and he longed for a
freedom that was not threatened. He longed to be united
with the God for whom he had suffered. There would at last
be an end to this persecution and cruelty. He was ready to
complete his journey, his pilgrimage and on August 31st,
1688, John Bunyan climbed the bank on the other side of the
river, and claimed his crown in the Celestial City.

It had been a life full of reckless activity and frustrating
inactivity. In the moments of freedom he had had to pack in
the life that he had lost in prison. He had never known his
own children as most parents know theirs. He had not
provided for them as well as his own parents had provided
for him; he had made his nearest and dearest suffer for his
beliefs.

He had begun in a tinker's small cottage and ended in the
house of a friend, far away from his home and family, just as
if he had died in prison. He was sixty years old; when he was

born the nation was on the verge of tyranny and revolution, when he died the nation was moving into a new era of freedom and tolerance. Few people can have contributed so much towards that tolerance as did John. Despite his early faltering towards salvation, once he discovered it, he proclaimed it and insisted on the right to uphold it. He articulated ideas and theologies that laid the foundations for the English Baptist movement in particular and the Non-Conformists in general, but most of all he wrote an epic story that the world today still reads in its millions. His contribution to English literature is as great as his contribution to the Christians of the world who find reflected in Pilgrim's story the stories of their own lives. A man who was ashamed of his profession, John succeeded in his own lifetime in overcoming that stigma and, although he became a celebrity then, he could not have guessed at the extent of his fame now. He was a forerunner of the freedom that he did not see, and the legacy he left has helped maintain and strengthen that tolerance and spread its influence worldwide.

Bibliography

By John Bunyan
Grace Abounding to the Chief of Sinners. Dent, 1970
The Holy War. Evangelical Press, 1976
The Life and Death of Mr Badman. Dent, 1970
The Pilgrim's Progress. Penguin, 1970
Some Gospel Truths Opened. Oxford University Press, 1980
Vindication of 'Some Gospel Truths Opened'. Oxford University Press, 1980

Brittain, Vera. *In the Steps of John Bunyan.* Rich and Cowan, 1951
Brockbank, E. *Edward Burrough.* The Bannisdale Press, 1949
Brown, John. *John Bunyan.* Wn. Isbister Limited
Diaries of Samuel Pepys, The. G. Bell, 1970–6
Foster, A.J. *Bunyan's Country.* H. Virtue & Co. Ltd., 1901
Fraser, Antonia. *Cromwell, Our Chief of Men.* Panther, 1975. *King Charles II.* Futura, 1981
Harrison, J.F.C. *The Common People.* Fontana, 1984
Hill, Christopher. *God's Englishman.* Penguin, 1972
Journals of George Fox, The. Friends Trust Association, Edward Hicks Jnr, 1891
Morrah, Patrick. *Restoration England.* Constable, 1979
Nicholson, John. *John Bunyan.* Essays into England No. 1, BM B020
Tibbutt, H.G. *What They Said About John Bunyan.* Beds County Council, 1981
Willcocks, M.R. *Bunyan Calling.* Allen & Unwin, 1944